How To Analyze People: A Practical Guide To Analyzing Body Language, Speed Reading People, And Increasing Emotional Intelligence & Protecting Against Dark Psychology & Manipulation

By Life Fulfilment Academy

Table of Contents

Introduction

Have you ever found yourself in an encounter with another person who left you wondering, "what the heck just happened?" Several years ago, I walked into my usual Friday hangout place. It was a lounge bar a few blocks from my home that offered live music on Friday evenings - a perfect way for me to reward myself after a long week of trying to meet deadlines and make customers happy. This particular Friday was different. Yes, the bartender waved and said hi, then gestured that he would be mixing up my "usual" and send it over to my table. And the pretty waitress that always comes to say hi still showed up did her flirty act as usual. That's not what was different. Instead, I'm talking about how I walked in one man, and by the end of the night; I was a completely different guy - dumbfounded and $2,000 short.

Whenever I've shared this story, people generally assume I was either robbed, I went to the casino and gambled then lost, or I was carrying cash in my wallet, and someone managed to blackmail me in some way. Actually, all those scenarios make a lot more sense than what I'm about to share. The fact is, no one robbed or blackmailed me, and I didn't gamble my money that Friday night. In fact, I didn't even have cash on me except for the taxi cash that I always have with me whenever I go out for a drink. So what the heck happened? Well, it all began when a very attractive woman captured my attention. What started as a brief conversation turned into one of the most exciting evenings of my life. She went from a complete stranger to me, wondering,

"Where have you been all my life?" At some point, I probably asked her out loud. We decided to move bars and go somewhere a bit less crowded and intimate. At her suggestion, we settled for a more upscale private lounge where we got to talking even more and grew even closer. By the end of the night, I wanted to take her home with me, but she seemed too dignified and perfect - I couldn't dare. We got into a taxi together, and as I dropped her home, I felt like it was the start of something that would last a lifetime. She said she couldn't wait to see me the next day when we were going to meet for dinner. I was already counting the hours. Back in my apartment, I tossed and turned as the night felt longer and longer. I didn't want to call in the middle of the night and come across desperate and weird, so instead, I lay on my bed, stared dreamily at my ceiling, and imagined the kind of romance that awaited me. It had been so long since I felt this way. I could see myself falling hard and fast, but it felt right because this woman got me. And just like that, consumed by my fiery passions of the new world that awaited me, I finally dozed off.

It must have been pretty late because the next morning, I awoke to the sound of a car alarm, which habitually went off when the neighborhood boys were pulling pranks or playing football on the street during the weekend. At that point, I am usually on my way out for my Saturday rounds. Today I had to nurse a mild hangover. But it didn't matter; my heart was pumped. The only thing ringing in my head was the timer I had set to call my date from last night to let her know what time I'd be picking her up. By the time it was finally acceptable to call her, I rang and got no answer. "*Hmmm. That's strange*," I thought to myself. So I waited for a few minutes and called again and again. Then I sent a text. Still no response. An hour went by, and ten unanswered calls later, I was starting to feel a bit frustrated.

By the time evening came, the idea of that romance had quickly turned into a hot mess. As I sat there on my couch looking staring blankly at my phone, I started to retrace the events of the previous evening to see if I was missing something. The bottom line, I was missing a lot! That entire evening that I felt was perfect turned out to be nothing more than a series of manipulation experiments that resulted in me spending two grand in both cash deposits and credit card payments. I realized I don't even recall what I was paying for. All I know is at the end of it all, I had a woman that seemed to have evaporated into thin air, and a few days later, her cell phone was disconnected.

There are many justifiable theories one might come up with, and trust me. I came up with a whole bunch. But at the end of the day, what that experience taught me is that in today's world, one has to be able to read people and protect himself or herself from those who seem to have a handle on dark manipulation. I've heard of cases that were worse than mine, where people have lost a lot more than two grand. But given how much my pride and bank account suffered that Friday night, I made it my mission to understand the psychology behind these twisted games and to help others avoid it.

There's nothing worse than falling victim to dark manipulation and being unable to detect it before its too late. Whether it's a business deal, a date, or any other interaction, I want to make sure those of us who are generous and empathetic get full protection against these toxic individuals who mean to harm us.

By reading this book, I assume you want to understand how to read people and protect yourself. My promise to you is that by the time you're through with this book, you'll be able to quickly analyze everyone around you whether in a professional or casual setting, and you'll also know how to see the real intentions people have as they approach you.

Why Learn How To Read Body Language

Reason #1: The first and foremost reason you should prioritize and train yourself to read body language and analyze people is that it will give you a skill set you can use for the rest of your life. That skill set will help you in personal and professional relationships.

Reason #2: Learning how to analyze people and read body language also enables you to increase self-awareness. As you'll get to learn shortly, your ability to read another depends on how well you can read and control your own body. Now, why would you care about controlling your own body language? That takes me to the next reason.

Reason #3: By learning to control your own body, you can quickly readjust yourself during a conversation. That will make you more likable and also give you the lead of where the conversation should go. Knowing how to adjust your body language to match that of another, you can quickly develop trust and empathy.

Reason #4: You will be able to protect yourself from manipulative people and narcissists. I have a lot of friends who are empaths, and this has been one of the most liberating skillset they learned. The more you can see through a person's intentions, the easier it will be to protect yourself from people who want to harm you. That is my intention for writing this book.

Reason #5: You will be able to control how others perceive you. If you don't know how you're carrying yourself, you might be sending off signals that attract narcissistic, toxic, or dangerous people. For example, I shared a story of you at the start of this book, where an attractive woman targeted me for her manipulative schemes. At first, it seemed so unfair, right? I felt it was unjust, and I certainly didn't deserve that level of psychological manipulation. However, as I started working on myself, it became evident that I was carrying myself around like a timid, desperate man. I probably portrayed weakness and low value. Each week I walked into my favorite hangout spot; I caused people to see me in a certain way. Perhaps that signal is what this woman spotted and decided to take action on.

How This Skill Will Protect You And Help You Succeed More In Your Professional Career.

Being able to read people is a skill that will protect you from negative or ill-intentioned people who only want to manipulate and take advantage of you. But there's another hidden advantage that I didn't realize until much later. The better you become at quickly analyzing people, the further you'll go in your career. Business is about people. Whether you are employed or running your own business, this skill will make you better at interacting with people. You'll learn what to look and listen for when dealing with people, whether they are colleagues, customers, potential investors, etc. Everybody is always communicating valuable signals to you. The words people speak may sometimes be masked, but their non-verbal cues never lie. Many experts agree that over sixty percent of our communication is non-verbal. Through understanding how to read facial expressions, posture, tone of voice, and other signals, you will have a better chance of seeing the real message being communicated to you at any given time. This book is here to simplify this process of mastering body language and speed reading people. I'm taking out complex ideas and jargon that most of us never understand, and I'm focusing on guiding you through a clear path of learning how to gain this all-important skill. If you're ready to start analyzing and speed-reading people, turn to the next chapter and let's begin with the basics.

Chapter 01: Why Does The Body React The Way It Does?

From the moment you are born to the moment you take your last breath, the only home you will ever inhabit is your body. Given how precious that body is, it makes sense that you should do everything possible to understand and take care of it. The best part is the more you know your body, the easier it becomes to understand other bodies and what they are secretly communicating.

Body Language

What is body language? The simplest way to describe it is that it is the non-verbal communication taking place between two interacting bodies. It is the unspoken element of communication that we use to express our true feelings far beyond what words can relay. Body language includes gestures, body posture, facial expressions, head, and eye movement.

Where Did Body Language Originate?

That's a great question, and I think the answer is that we've been communicating with our bodies long before we could write. In fact, we can trace body language communication all the way back to our closest ancestors - the chimpanzees. Research scientists have proven chimpanzees not only communicate, but they also share similar emotions to humans. Dr. Jane Goodall teaches a Master class on the conversation and way of communication that she discovered takes place among the Chimpanzee community. Regardless of which species you study, the bottom line is that we all developed body language as a means of communication in the past. As we advanced and developed, we phased out certain actions and innovated new ones to help us better communicate and express our feelings and thoughts. Whether you're thinking about non-human body language communication such as how male gorillas stand up on two legs beating their chest as a sign of dominance or how primates bear teeth to communicate aggression or even how modern human beings send out emojis instead of words to pass on a message these are all non-verbal signals that are meant to help us all express our current feelings and intentions.

While anyone can learn to read these signs, few have been trained to consciously do it or even use it proactively to their own benefit. Learning how to read body language, however, must begin with oneself. Unless you increase your awareness and understand what your own body is communicating, you don't stand a chance at effectively understanding what other bodies are telling you. So the first lesson is going to be, learning to decipher what your body is telling you, figuring out how you carry your own body and why you've been sending off the signals you usually send out.

Understanding What The Body Is Telling You

People are always communicating their true feelings through non-verbal cues, and so do you. Are you aware of what signals your body is sending as you interact with others? If you think about it, body language can help you become what others call psychic or a mind reader because you'll be able to tell if someone is sincere, lying, pretending, or bothered by something at any given moment. There are many clues you can start looking out for as you interact with other people. I also encourage you to monitor yourself for the next seven days. Place a mirror where you eat, sleep, and lounge to see how you carry yourself. If it's at all possible, record yourself while working or in a meeting. Then take time to reflect on how you felt and what your body was saying during those moments. A few signals you can immediately start looking out for include:

• The body posture of another as well as your own.

• The smile on someone's face. Can you seek the corner of the eyes wrinkle and fold as the person smiles? Experts tell us that a real smile often creates a natural crinkle around the eyes.

• Is someone sneering while you speak? Are their eyes shifting all over the place? Do they seem constricted and "closed" in as they talk to you or open and relaxed?

These are just a few of the body signals you need to start noticing because they are all communicating something about that particular interaction. Why should this matter to you? Because the more you understand how others perceive you, the more you can control that perception. It's also the best way to ensure you come across as friendly, confident, and likable. Another added benefit of this is that you'll be able to tell when someone is faking it with you. For example, my sister recently caught his boyfriend flirting with another woman. The guy apologized, and it seemed pretty heartfelt, but my sister could see in his eyes and from his body language that he wasn't sincere. She ended the relationship immediately after because she didn't want to wait a year of being in a relationship with a man who was obviously not that serious about being faithful. Think of the heartache she just saved herself by calling it off earlier in the game before things got too messy. That is the power of having this skill set and using it effectively.

Throughout this book, we'll dive deeper into signals and how you can start interpreting them.

Human Reflex, Inevitable, Or Not?

When an infant first sees a burning candle, the fascination of the fire usually causes them to reach out and touch it. I'm sure we've all had that same urge. But you and I both know our reflexes would kick in as soon as we attempted the foolish move of touching something hot like a burning candle flame. Yet the infant is most likely to end up getting burned because, for some reason, their brain doesn't register any action. Why is that?

Reflexes are there to protect us from danger. As we grow older, our reflexes get better, and we develop automatic responses that do not require the brain to create or direct any new action. Think of how fast you move your finger when you mistakenly touch a hot pan. What about when someone is about to slam the car door on your poor fingers? You'll most likely pull your hand away super fast. That reaction is natural and very good because it's meant to protect you from losing your fingers or getting burned etc. These types of involuntary responses, also known as reflexes, occur very quickly (most of them faster than the blink of an eye). But how do they work?

For your reflexes to work, there must be excellent internal communication.

Your reflexes affect your body posture and sense of balance as well as coordination in more ways than you previously imagined. When your reflexes are working well, it's easy to maintain a strong body posture even without much conscious attention. On the flip side, if you have a dysfunctional reflex, then it might take a lot of conscious effort to maintain proper balance, body posture, and coordination. From the moment you were born, learned to hold your neck up straight, sit, stand, and eventually walk, your reflexes have been working to stabilize your spine and, in turn, your posture. Posture is the reflexive anti-gravitational adaptation of the living body so it can function efficiently in the environment it lives in. In your case, the kind of posture you have depends on reflex actions that happen as the result of many different sensory input integrations. These, in turn, create rapid motor reactions involving the visual, proprioceptive, and vestibular systems. When any of these three systems are out of whack, you'll notice you have difficulty with coordination, controlling eye movements, controlling your posture, and you might even experience a lot of anxiety and fear.

As you can see, this can be an inhibiting factor if you want to learn how to analyze and read people's body language. When you have trouble controlling your body, it's going to be tough reading that of another. There's also the common challenge that many of us unconsciously struggle with, whereby our bodies fall under the influence or control of primitive reflexes that no longer serve us. In such cases, individuals will find themselves overreacting, lacking the ability to control and automate the processing of simple movements and tasks. When that occurs, you'll notice the person appear overly nervous or "jerky" in his or her movement—for example, accidentally pouring a coffee in hand over a person instead of calmly stretching out your hand for a handshake. The bottom line is, you need to make sure your reflexes aren't working against you. If they are, that's the first change you need to make.

Breaking Down The Human Body

The body is complex, and there are many ways to approach understanding body language. In this chapter, we focus on the exciting science behind body language. I've simplified it to make sure you don't get bored with all the boring stuff.

Kinesics

This refers to body language or body movements in scientific terms. That includes gestures, head and hand movements, body posture, and whole-body movement. When we use our body, we can emphasize or reinforce what we are saying as well as better express a particular emotion or attitude. For example, suppose someone asked you how your recent trip to Russia was, and you stood up from your chair, and then animatedly moved your body, shivering as if you were freezing. That person now has a much better sense of what you experienced. You could have easily said, "it was cold," and that would be that. However, by including full-body movement and emotion, the person got a much better sense of how cold the experience was for you. That is a simple example of how we use body movement to communicate. However, not all people match their words with their body movements. In a later chapter, we'll dive more into this, but for now, realize that the more you become skillful at reading people, you might start to detect inconsistencies in behavior that you didn't catch prior to reading this book. Being able to spot such discrepancies will help you know what someone is really thinking and feeling. Let's dive deeper into the various types of body movements. These include illustrators, emblems, regulators, adaptors, posture, and mirroring.

Illustrators - These are gestures that accompany words to illustrate a verbal message. The example of shivering in cold as you describe your Russian trip is an example of an illustrator. Another example would be making circular motion movements with your hands as you say the phrase "over and over again."

Emblems - These are gestures that serve the same function as a word. For example, Italians use a lot of emblems in their conversations, and in the American culture, we have hand movements that show you want to hitch a ride or that you're summoning someone to call you. Depending on culture, emblems will vary, so make sure you use the right one to avoid miscommunication.

Regulators - These are gestures that give feedback to a person during a conversation. It helps you show interest and agreement or disagreement when engaging with someone else. Suppose you're having a conversation with a boss or family member. As they speak, you'll want to give feedback and let them know that you're paying attention by either nodding your head or making short sounds such as uh-huh. These are both examples of regulators.

Adaptors - These are non-verbal behaviors that a person usually does without conscious awareness. Most of the time, it will be a physical act that often reveals feelings of anxiety, nervousness, or even hostility. If you notice someone biting his or her fingernails (or if you bite your nails), that's an adaptive behavior indicating you're nervous. Someone might scratch, shake their legs, or adjust their glasses. Some girls are known to bite their hair or even twirl it around their fingers. These are all examples of adaptive behavior, trying to satisfy some psychological and physical needs.

Posture - Later in this book, we'll talk more about posture and the two main types of postures you need to become aware of (including their meaning), but for now, understand that posture is extremely important when analyzing people. Posture reflects emotions, attitudes, and even intentions. When you learn to read the cues someone's posture demonstrates, you can easily interpret hidden emotions, information, and personality without ever asking the other person what they want.

Mirroring - This is the ability to reflect what someone is showing you. Babies are professionals at imitation and mirroring what they see from their mom. If you observe two lovers sitting across a table having dinner, you'll also observe this mirroring effect. Mirroring is such a powerful tool to learn and then use because it enables you to express empathy, which instantly creates a bond. Mirroring usually indicates interest and makes the other person feel like "you get them."

Oculesics

This refers to the study of eye behavior and the non-verbal communication the eyes are attempting to relay. Think of it as a subcategory of kinesics (the study of body language). In this branch, we attempt to interpret and understand eye movement, eye behavior, gaze, and everything your eyes might be conveyed in a secret code. Let's look at the main factors that are studied in oculesics.

Length of the duration of eye contact

Ever had someone stare at you for a minute too long to the point where it became unnatural? They went from being confident to bring creepy, right? Well, the thing with length of duration of eye contact is that depending on which culture you're dealing with, you're going to have varying experiences. In the West, we associate direct eye contact with honey. If someone can look you in the eyes while talking, they are generally honest and kind. Move to the African culture, and things become shifty. If you're having a conversation with someone and they lower their gaze that implies humility. Easy to make assumptions, right?

If you thought that was too much, head over to China, and chances are you won't make any friends there if you give them straight and confident eye contact. The Chinese associate too much eye contact with rudeness. What?

So, when it comes to an understanding of the duration of eye contact, how long is too long? According to experts at Scientific America, the average and most comfortably accepted length is around 3 seconds. Yeah, that little. If you stretch to 4, then you start bordering on weird at best and intimidating or threatening at worst. Your take-home point is to be mindful of the environment, culture, and the people you're interacting with to determine how much eye contact and for how long.

Direction

We consider it a good sign when someone looks right into our eyes, yes? And we assume that if someone is looking away or down, it's because they are processing something. We've come to these commonly accepted interpretations because, over time, we learned that when someone is interested in us, they would direct their eyes toward us. That is accurate. But how can you interpret other directional movements such as looking left, down, etc.? Well, experts suggest that for the most part looking down could be a sign of submissiveness, guilt, or disinterest depending on the environment and culture. Looking towards the lateral left indicates an effort to recall a song or sound, whereas looking in the upper left direction generally implies the person might be trying to fetch a visual memory recently stored.

If someone is talking to himself or herself or engaged in deep thought, they will most likely look toward their lower left. If the person is creating a visual image of something, they will mostly shift in the direction of the upper right corner of their eyes. People who often lie tend to move their eyes to look towards their lateral right. Observe how often you notice this when talking to someone, and you might just witness a potential lie in the making.

Eye movement

We interpret someone's eye movement and determine how they are feeling in various ways, most of which we've come to associate with basic human instinct. For example, someone will cover his or her eyes to indicate discomfort. Although sunglasses are considered fashionable and cool, the main reason a person wears glasses is to eliminate or manage discomfort. If you see someone blocking their eyes, rubbing them, or excessively blinking, that could be a sign that they're taking in bad news. Experts on this subject matter also tell us that darting eyes usually indicated that the person feels insecure and is looking for an escape from that ongoing conversation. And of course, when someone squints, that implies they are suspicious of something.

Pupil Intensity

One last thing you want to start observing is the intensity of the pupil when talking to someone. Experts say that, in general, mydriasis will occur when a person is interested in whatever they are engaged in. Mydriasis is the medical term for pupil dilation. So if you're talking to someone you care about and you notice their eyes brighten up, and their pupil dilate, you can be sure they are very interested in keeping that conversation going. If, on the other hand, you notice someone's pupil constrict, it's likely that they are not interested and perhaps even feel offended by the current engagement. While this isn't an exact science since we know that pupil dilation is light dependant, which means it may not happen for every individual in that exact way, it's a good habit to at least pay attention to the overall intensity of a person's pupil as you engage in conversation. You never know what those eyes might reveal.

Haptics

This refers to the study of our sense of touch in medical, biological, or technological applications. Both haptics and proxemics (we'll talk about that next) deal with personal space and territory. Touch is only possible when we allow others to enter our intimate space or when we enter someone's personal space. Done correctly, a single moment of touching another can generate a bonding effect that can prove very advantageous. This isn't just theory; it's been verified to work in real-world scenarios. For example, in Vanessa Van Edward's blog, she provides a story that you can supposedly find on the television series called "How 2 Win". While I haven't watched the series, she talked about the episode where science journalist Jeff Wise ran an experiment with a man named Vincent. Vincent was introduced to random people in the park, where he shook their hand, smiled, and said, "Hi, nice to meet you!" After Vincent was taken out of sight, Wise went in to gather feedback from the strangers who mostly rated him a five or a six! That's not very impressive. Imagine if he was trying to get hired for a job. The second part of the experiment involved Vincent saying exactly the same thing, dressing exactly the same way, keeping the same facial expression, etc. He was basically the same but with one new add-on. This time around the feedback from the second group was incredible. Most people rated him an 8 or 9! But he hadn't changed anything, or had he?

Actually, he had made one small adjustment, and that was - his handshake. In the first experiment, Vincent used a standard one-handed handshake. In the second experiment, he involved his other hand and used it to touch the forearm of the other person lightly. That small shift made all the difference in how people perceived him as a first impression. I share this to emphasize the importance of learning when to use touch appropriately. Human contact is scientifically proven to release oxytocin, which in turn makes us feel more strongly connected to the other individual. Most of the time, this happens at a subconscious level, and so what we want to ensure is that we are able to detect it from others quickly, and we also want to know the best time for us to do it.

Your skin is the largest organ, and it is continuously receiving and deciphering information from your environment. Therefore touch is very emotional and volatile. Touch can be used as a therapeutic tool, an amplifier, or as a means of forming a connection with another. Used properly, it creates an instant connection; used poorly, it can quickly backfire. So let's talk about the types of touch you should know about.

Holding hands - is a form of touching. We commonly interpret it as a symbol of unity and trust. It can be done between friends and/or lovers. Of course, holding hands should only be done in the right context, so make sure you are only attempting to do it with the right person.

Hugs - are great. We all know them; many of us love them, while some of us don't. They can happen between friends, colleagues, family members, and lovers. But how do you do it, right? You can either go for a pat or a platonic hug, which is short and casual when you don't want to imply something romantic by it. The slower and longer it is, the more you run the risk of coming off as sexually-oriented, especially if you're giving it to someone who is not a family member. As for the pat (usually two pats on the back), use it when you're avoiding too much physical proximity. Because most of the time, a pat is a signal that it's time to let go or that one isn't that interested in getting intimate. So if a girl you like ever "pats you on the back," she's sending you a message loud and clear.

Other types of hugs include the bro-hug, which is a combination of a handshake and a platonic hug where maximum distance, especially around the hip area, is maintained. There's also the side hug, which is also quite neutral. It can be used in a group setting or when you're trying to create affinity with a potential partner. But if you use this hug in the early stages of pursuing someone you like, make sure you don't dwell there too long as you might end up stuck in the "friendzone." One thing to note about the position of the hands during this friendly side hug is where someone places their hand. If you notice the hand wrapped around the neck, it's ordinarily indicative of dominance over that person sending a message of "ownership," so take note of where someone places their hand on you the next time this happens. The other kind of hug you might often see, especially when a lover is trying to send a strong message, is the "behind the back" type of hug. A lover will usually approach their partner from behind and encircle them with their hands. Depending on the context, this could just be an expression of affection, i.e., something the couple likes to do, or it could be a signal to the imminent threat that has been detected. But in all cases, this is a demonstration that the two are involved. The last type of hug is the criss-cross hug, which is extremely intimate and perfect for lovers, especially as a set-up for a passionate kiss. In this type of hug, one hand rests on the waist, and the other goes up to around the neck or shoulder, creating an X. Only do this with someone who enjoys being deeply intimate with you and also, make sure they are comfortable being that up close because some people don't like this type of hug. A key thing to remember is that the position of the hand does matter. If someone is hugging you, where they place their hand will help you understand the message they are attempting to communicate. A good rule of thumb is the more platonic the hug, the more the hands will be around the shoulders, or crossing underneath the arms and around the upper back. The more romantic the gesture, the closer the hands will be around the more intimate regions such as the waist. The distance between you and the other person will be less, and your most intimate areas will come into closer contact.

Kissing - is also a form of touch that has many meanings. In some cultures, like in Italy, kissing is part of everyday greetings. It's not only reserved for family members or lovers. In other parts of the world, it is considered a form of intimacy that should only be practiced between lovers behind closed doors. Again, it all comes back to understanding the culture and environment you're in before interpreting or attempting to use this form of touch. So yes, kissing has a lot to do with context and status; therefore, let's briefly talk about some of the kissing types you might want to learn to interpret. Kissing on the hand, especially when a man does it to a woman, is usually a sign of admiration. When you see a member of an Italian mob kissing the don's hand or ring, this is typically a sign of respect and submission. You might also see a petitioner kissing the hand of a priest or even the pope in a religious setting, which indicates honor and respect. This type of non-verbal cue, in general, suggests that the participants are not equal in status, which is why it typically involves one party bowing or lowering their head and chest area. Then there's the other type of kiss where someone kisses from above instead of bowing. Think of it like when your mom or dad or grandparent wants to soothe you in some way. Usually, this type of kiss is on the forehead and represents protection, nurturing, and patronage. Lastly, there's the kiss on the cheek, which can be interpreted as mutual respect because it takes place on equal ground. Other types of readings you can observe is when someone kisses an inanimate object. This is usually a sign of admiration, gratefulness, or a religious symbol of respect. Of course, this section would be incomplete if I didn't at least help you analyze the difference between a platonic kiss where someone isn't sending you a hidden message vs. when they are.

To effectively read a kiss, some of the things you want to look for is how tensed up the lips are as they kiss you on the cheek, for example. Are they puckered up or loose and relaxed? Was the kiss right in the middle of the cheek? Was it an air kiss? When someone is kissing you with no hidden agenda, they will usually kiss the middle of the cheek, and it will be with puckered lips. On the other hand, if the kisser is trying to lead you on or send a message, the kiss might be closer to the mouth or closer to the ear, and the lips will be more relaxed, making the kiss softer and lasting a moment longer than usual. They might also gently caress your cheek with theirs intentionally as they move away from your face or even blow a little air toward your ear as they move out of the kiss, signaling something passionate awaits.

Proxemics

This refers to the study of personal space. You cannot understand proxemics without diving into the understanding of culture and the impact it has on body language. Why? Because personal space and "closeness" will vary from one culture to the next. Depending on where you grew up, your perception of personal space and closeness will differ from someone who grew up on the other side of the planet. For example, Italians and Spanish cultures have a very different approach to Japanese culture. I would imagine it would require a different approach if you want to master the right body language and how to interact with people in Japan. It's essential to keep this in mind as you mix and mingle in our multicultural society. If you violate someone else's idea of "appropriate" distance, you'll have a hard time making friends or positively influencing that interaction. In the East, things are very different as compared to the West, where we grew up. Here in the West, we've identified four main categories of proxemics. The intimate distance where being close is perfectly normal can be anything from physical touching to 54cm. Personal distance is anything between 45com to 1.2m. The social distance (where one needs a lot more space) is anything between 1.2m to 3.6m, and lastly, public distancing is between 3.7m to 4.5m. Where did we get these categories? They are based on the four types of relationships we have in our society.

Intimate relations - is the one I call intimate distancing, which ranges from close physical contact to 45cm. It should only be with someone you have a close relationship with.

Personal relations - is considered most appropriate for people holding a conversation. This is where handshaking is possible, and you can easily see the expressions and eye movements of the person you're interacting with. It's also easy to see their whole body language.

Social relations - is the average distance for impersonal business. Think of you and a co-worker or you and a fellow networker sitting in a conference or seminar event. In such cases, whether you are sitting across a desk or table from another or in an event room, with social distancing, the speech has to be louder, and eye contact must be intentionally maintained to communicate effectively.

Public relations - is the acceptable distance for general and impersonal interactions. A teacher in a class or a speaker at a conference usually addresses the group at a public distance range. At this range, exaggerated non-verbal communication is necessary; otherwise, interest will drop. If you're addressing people at this range, you would need larger head movements, precise hand gestures, and an increased tone of voice to effectively communicate and keep the attention of your listener.

Chapter 02: Is What He's Saying The Same To What He's Actually Doing?

Now that you understand a bit more about your body and the different ways it relays information, it's time to start applying that knowledge in your interaction with other people. After all, the human experience is only enriched when we engage, interact, and share moments with another. In the previous chapter, I touched on how sometimes you might start to notice that one's body movement doesn't seem to match their actions. This is one of the advantages you'll get as you master the skill of analyzing people. Some people will say things they don't mean either to hide insecurities or to mask their true intentions. You want to avoid falling for these traps because even if someone is doing it for a good reason, it's essential to protect yourself from deceit and false communication. A huge component of getting good at spotting these inconsistencies in someone, whether it's a professional or personal encounter, is to dive deeper into the different ways we communicate so you can learn to pay attention to the signals that are usually present.

How Humans Communicate

Communication is the act of sharing information from one person to another or a group of people. We have been passing on information as long as our species has been alive. That is the only way we've been able to survive. Over millennia our way of passing on information has evolved and become more sophisticated. Nonetheless, this isn't something new or foreign to your human nature. You already know how to communicate effectively. But there's a difference between basic instincts and high-level mastery. In this book, you're learning to become a master at an art that's integral to human survival. Let's take a closer look at the four primary communication types that we use and how you can immediately start strengthening your skills for each of them.

Verbal Communication

Verbal communication is the use of language to transfer information. This can be done through voice or sign language. It's is the most common type of communication our society uses for both personal and professional interactions. When you take a language course to learn Spanish or French, what you're implying there is that you want to communicate with the people of that culture verbally.

In our modern society, verbal communication has been upgraded to go beyond physical interactions. With the use of technology and the Internet, we can do phone calls, online presentations, one-on-one meetings, podcasting, and voice recordings to share with people who are on the other side of the planet from us. The creation of voice technology such as Google Home and Alexa is also demonstrating that we are taking verbal communication to the next level because not only are we communicating with fellow human beings, we are now starting to hold voice conversations with artificial intelligence. That's a whole other topic, but I'm bringing it to your attention so you can realize the importance of strengthening your ability to use verbal communication effectively. Before we can talk about how to read the verbal cues of another, let's see how you can immediately work to strengthen how you communicate verbally.

• Speak confidently, use a firm, clear voice, and avoid filler words. This is especially important when using technology but also when in front of a person or group of people listening to you. Be precise with your words as much as possible and avoid filler words such as um, so, yeah, etc.

• Listen with intention. This is known as active listening and is just as crucial to your verbal communication. The better you become at listening to others as they communicate, the more you'll grow as a communicator, and you'll actually hear what they really mean.

Non-verbal Communication

Non-verbal implies the use of body language, as we've discussed so far in this book. It can be used consciously and unconsciously. Many people have no idea what their eyes or hands are doing as they speak. For example, if you're the type of person who gets really nervous and bites their fingernails unconsciously. You might unintentionally start biting your fingernails when you hear unpleasant information, even if it's not appropriate. Getting to understand non-verbal communication is one of the best ways to analyze and read people because body language always tells the real feelings and thoughts that someone is experiencing at that moment. A few things you can immediately do to start strengthening this skill include:

•Pay attention to what you're feeling. At many points during the day and especially when engaging in conversations, both positive and negative, take a pause and internally do a check-in. Become aware of what happens to your emotions.

• Notice how those emotions feel physically. Once you do a check-in, notice how that gets projected to your physical body. Does your chest tighten up? Does your throat dry up? Does your stomach feel tight if you're feeling anxious? What about when you're feeling happy? Does your posture change in any way? This level of self-awareness is crucial if you want to gain mastery over how you show up in the world.

• Mimic non-verbal cues that prove to be effective. You will notice that certain body language movements and facial expressions are beneficial to a certain environment. Take these little lessons and implement them in your communication. For example, if you realize that a particular friend or your boss nods their head in approval whenever they want to communicate positive feedback, do the same. Take that same approach, and in your next encounter, when you wish to show approval and positive feedback, make sure you nod.

Visual Communication

Visual communication involves using art, photographs, drawings, sketches, charts, and graphs to convey information. They are extremely beneficial when combined with written and/or verbal communication. In our tech-focused society, visual communication has seen a growing trend thanks to social media platforms like Instagram. I am inclined to think more and more people will continue to use this style of communication to consume ideas, share information, etc. A few ways you can start to improve on this type of communication include:

• Consider expressing yourself more with emojis, graphics, and other types of imagery, as long as they are appropriate for the situation.

• In your formal communications such as emails, presentations, etc. you may add visuals to help express your message. Just be sure to include visuals that are easy to understand.

Written Communication

The last form of communication we are going to discuss is written communication, which involves typing, printing symbols or handwriting numbers, letters, and symbols. Written communication is prevalent in our society, as we have been doing it for a long time through traditional means. Today we do it through letters, emails, social media posts, blogs, newspapers, books, and the list goes on and on. Being a great communicator with words requires a lot of practice and skill. If you want to get better, here are a few things to implement.

• Be clear and concise with the words you choose. Keep things simple and be mindful of the meaning the reader will perceive as they consume your communication.

• Read as much as you can from authors, bloggers, poets, and other writers that you enjoy. The more you read, the better you'll be at writing something that another person enjoys. It will also help you learn how to effectively utilize tone of voice, humor, sarcasm, etc.

Exchanging Information With Verbal Communication

As you might have understood by now, we are constantly exchanging information, advice, and our state of being whether we use spoken, written, or non-verbal means of communication. I want us to dive deeper into the nature of how this exchange takes place for both verbal and non-verbal.

Contrary to what you might have heard, verbal and non-verbal are meant to work hand in hand. The fact that we misalign them and end up creating conflict is an error on our part. According to Wertheim, a researcher on this topic, nob-verbal communication is meant to do one of the following: Reinforce, substitute, contradict, accentuate, or regulate what you're communicating.

Let's take a closer look at the nature of verbal communication, which has become our most relied upon form of communication. This is, of course, done through spoken or written words. If you're speaking, then that includes the tone of your voice and word choice. If you're writing, you can also express "your voice," but it's a lot harder to do when writing than speaking. Whether you realize it or not, whenever you've interacted with another human being at a social gathering, you are continually giving off and receiving certain signals. You must become more aware of the signs you are giving off either through your tone of voice, body language behavior, and even how you write (yes, that includes your instant messenger chats)—more on that in an upcoming chapter. Let's discuss some of the characteristics of both verbal and non-verbal communication.

With verbal communication that would include:

• The structured use of words. That means you need to follow the rules of grammar and put together words that give clear messages.

• Mostly consciously chosen. Each word in verbal communication has a distinct meaning, which means when we speak or write, we deliberately select the word to use based on the meaning we intend to share. That eliminates the high risk of misinterpretation.

• Left-brain work. The left hemisphere of the brain, where reasoning and analysis take place, interprets verbal stimuli.

• Distance doesn't matter. That's true for almost all verbal communication styles, which is why we can call, send emails, write letters, do online conferences, etc.

• Communication is fast, efficient, and easy to generate evidence and/or witnesses.

With non-verbal communication that would include:
• No use of words. That means you don't need to use any language, oral, or written.

• Largely unconscious. For many people, the messages are passed on without conscious control of the individual because most people have no self-awareness. They don't know what expression their face is making as they interact with another etc.

• Right brain work. That means the right hemisphere is the one responsible for interpreting the communication, which involves spatial, pictorial, gestalt activities in the bran and creates responses.

• Expresses feelings, attitudes, and intentions. That's primarily because eyes, body movements, and gestures all communicate emotions and attitude whether the person realizes or not.

• Distance really matters. That's because the only way to read someone's body language is through face-to-face interactions.

• Communication is highly subjective and, at times, can be more time consuming to pass on, especially if the receiving party doesn't "get it." It's also highly subjective and makes it hard to show evidence that you have passed on a particular communication. In a group setting, it's also very open to individual interpretation because everyone will perceive what they want.

• Purely informal. That's due to the fact that non-verbal communication doesn't really follow any rules. It's also influenced heavily by the culture of a place, which means different gestures might have different meanings depending on where you are in the world. For example, in America, steady eye contact is considered a good thing. The same thing in China would be regarded as a bad thing. In the west, we nod our heads up and down for agreement, but if you go to India, they won't interpret it the same way because they nod in agreement using a totally different body movement.

Paying Attention To The Non-Verbal Communication

Actions speak louder than words is an only proverb that holds real meaning if you want to become an effective communicator. That's why you really should pay attention to the non-verbal signals you give off as well as those that others give you. Researchers in communication suggest that more feelings and true intentions are sent and received non-verbally than verbally. If you think about it, this makes sense. I am certain that any narcissist or manipulative person can be easily detectable by you once you learn how to read their body language. Later in this book, I'll help you become a pro at that. Why, though, should you pay more attention to non-verbal communication? Well, aside from the fact that it is the best way to protect yourself against toxic people, manipulative and ill-intentioned people, it's also one of the best skills you can develop to help you succeed in life. The better you become at controlling your body language and reading other people, the easier it will be to resonate with the people you want to resonate with.

Let's assume you have been dreaming of getting promoted from junior to a senior-level manager at your company. For a while now, you feel like your boss has been overlooking you because he just doesn't "get you." He can't seem to see the talent and value you bring to the table. What do you do? By improving your non-verbal communication skills, you can learn to analyze him quickly to figure out how to best communicate with him. In so doing, you'll be able to create the kind of rapport needed and demonstrate the level of confidence and competency he's looking for, thereby assuring your promotion. The same is true whether you want a girl to go out with you, sell a customer into buying your product, or even getting your spouse to agree on something. The more you can pay attention to non-verbal communication and understand what people really want, the easier it becomes to build a rapport that works in your favor.

The signs you want to look for are those quick messages and expressions they are communicating to you as you interact. Look out for the hidden meaning or the real communication your counterpart is projecting at any given moment through their gestures, facial expressions, and another body movement. As you do this, though, I want you to become ever so mindful of the situation and the cultural context you're in. It's not just about learning to interpret a sign or symbol; it's about recognizing what it means for that person. For example, if you're engaging with someone in Africa, pay attention to how they use their eyes. When you observe them lowering their gaze and hardly making eye contact, don't just assume they are lying or disinterested. Be mindful of what that particular non-verbal communication means to them and then make a judgment through that perspective. As an American, your first reaction might be to assume you're dealing with the wrong person. But once you realize that lowered eye gaze is a sign of humility and submission, that changes everything. So pay attention but do it mindfully with the proper context of the environment.

Avoiding Miscommunication

This chapter would surely be incomplete if we failed to discuss the all-important issue of cultural influence on non-verbal communication. In many cases, miscommunication, both verbally and non-verbally, occurs when people don't understand each other. Verbally it's a result of not speaking the same language. Although most of the world speaks English, we have to recognize that Italians, Germans, Spanish, Arabic, Russian, Turkish, Portuguese, French, Chinese, Japanese, and Swahili speakers all use it as their second or third language. That creates a lot of room for miscommunication and poor understanding. When an American lands in China, if he or she doesn't speak Chinese and he comes across a village where no one speaks a word of English, all the communication the American might give will be worthless as the people of that village will not understand it. To make verbal communication even more complicated, we need to acknowledge the difference in dialects and accents within nations, even if their language is the same. For example, many of us don't know this, but the Italian language has many different accents and dialects. In fact, people in the Northern part of Italy consider themselves very different from people in the Southern part of Italy. If you were to spend enough time with two Italians (one from the north and the other from the south), it would soon become evident that these two people though both Italians are different. They use different words, accents, and dialects. In some cases, a word would have a different meaning as well. You'll see the same phenomenon in many other countries.

Even here in the United States, we can tell when someone is from Texas or when he's from Boston. How? Because of the accent and dialect of the English language. Aside from the main spoken and written languages, we also have to become aware of the simplified language (pidgin) that many of us use to chat. LOL used to mean Lots Of Love before it converted to mean Laugh Out Loud. If someone sends me "LOL," I'm often confused because, based on my understanding, it could mean either. So when it comes to using pidgin and abbreviations, please make sure you are very clear about the meaning you want to convey.

On the other hand, non-verbal communication can also create a lot of misunderstanding if done in the wrong context. For example, did you know that a smile in Russia is considered a bad thing? If you just walk up and smile to a stranger in most parts of the world, that would be considered a good thing - except in Russia. So don't do it. The biggest handicap that I see with non-verbal communication is the fact that it's culture-bound. Gestures that we consider positive in the American culture might be interpreted as obscene in other cultures. The fact that it requires someone who "gets you" also makes it easy for misunderstanding to creep in. People who don't prefer to use this form of communication or those that have inadequate or false meanings attached to a particular gesture or facial expression might quickly become offended. As such, I do not recommend using it as a public tool for communication unless you know your audience well enough.

Before moving on to the next chapter, here are some tips on how you can avoid miscommunication and language barriers.

• Educate yourself on cultural differences. The first thing you need to do, whether you are engaging a person or a group of people for the first time, is to try to understand their environment and culture as much as possible. That may include everything from the way people sit in their chairs to the way they speak to one another. You want to make sure you don't come across as rude, insensitivity, or ill-intention in any way. The same is true when you are faced with a situation that makes you feel unsure about what someone really means. Take your time to research a bit about the person before jumping into an over reactive conclusion.

• Use simple language. I find this to be the best way to avoid miscommunicating, especially around people who don't know you very well. The simpler the word choice and/or body language, which leaves little room for misinterpretation, the better. For example, if you're speaking to a group or Spanish speakers, using American idioms and metaphors to pass on a message is probably not a good idea. Most people will confuse the meaning, which might lead to miscommunication.

• Be mindful of the gestures you use. That goes back to understanding the context and environment you're in. Some of the gestures we consider normal like a thumbs up might be offensive in other places, so learn to regulate and control your body language. That way, you can quickly adapt to new environments and avoid creating unnecessary conflict.

• Work on your confidence. Often a lack of confidence or shyness can create room for misunderstanding. You might come across as incompetent, disrespectful, or suspicious even if that couldn't be further away from the truth.

• Be precise about the words and non-verbal cues you will use before expressing yourself. Before trying to get your point across to others, make sure you're clear on what you want to convey and why. Arranging your thoughts and determining your emotional state before communicating either verbally or non-verbally will enable you to express yourself clearly and succinctly. It will also help you stay on point and ensure you get the full attention of the receiver.

• Become an active listener. This is a big one if you want to become more effective with verbal communication. As simple as it may sound, listening is surprisingly hard for many of us. Most people aren't listening; they are waiting for the other person to stop talking so they can start talking. Unless you actively listen to the other person, it's going to be hard to grasp the real meaning they are trying to convey. And if you do a poor job getting the message, you'll likely interpret it poorly. I encourage you to actively listen whenever someone is talking to you and don't be afraid to ask them to repeat or explain further if at all, you don't get what they mean.

• Become an active observer. Just as we have mentioned with active listening, you also need to be more present and mindful of your environment and your counterpart. What is their posture, what expressions are they making, and what does that mean based on the current setting? With this knowledge, you can make discern the right message that is being conveyed, whether it is obvious or not.

• If you want to avoid miscommunication, you need to watch your tone and body language. That's why you'll see throughout this book I keep emphasizing increasing your self-awareness. If you're unconsciously giving off the wrong signals or unintentionally using the wrong facial expression, body language, volume, and tone of voice, it's easy to create conflict misunderstandings. This is what the next chapter will help you avoid or completely eliminate. Keep turning the pages to learn how to keep your emotions in check, control your body language, and build up your confidence.

Chapter 03: How The World Sees You

Back in college, I had a friend in my senior year that struggled to communicate in front of large groups and especially in front of girls. He was the only guy I knew who never had a date to the movies or the pool parties. He came in alone, stayed alone, and left alone. The guy was brilliant and very charming once you got to know him, but I guess the world wasn't seeing that side of him, which is why no one ever gave him a chance.

This one time, he applied for an internship at a company he really wanted to work for and made it all the way to the interview. Knowing how smart and hardworking he is, it was a no brainer for me. I was sure he was more qualified than any of the interviewees. Yet the interviewer didn't buy into it. I asked him why he thought they didn't accept his application, and he said, " *they loved everything I had submitted. It's the final interview that let me down. I sat there frozen like a dumb person as this lady asked me question after question. She was so puzzled that I had submitted the application, given my in-person experience. Even though I wanted to say so much, I just couldn't. It's like something was holding me back.*"

Poor kid struggled with the very thing I want us to address in this chapter. He was right. Something was holding him back. I don't want you to experience that same anguish.

Do You Really See Yourself When You Look In The Mirror?

Whenever we struggle to express ourselves confidently, we can almost always tie it back to low self-esteem and lack of enough self-love. Most of us just don't love ourselves enough. I don't mean vanity type of love; I mean deep unconditional love. To love yourself, you must know yourself.

I know a lot of guys who struggle to keep healthy, loving relationships, and they have all kinds of reasons for it (in fact, I used to be one of those guys). Regardless of the excuse, you might have, the fact remains that you can't ever attract and keep the love of another when you don't know how to love yourself. And you can't know how to love yourself if you don't have a working relationship with yourself. Have you ever taken yourself out on a date just to explore more about yourself, likes, dislikes, etc.? If that sounds too strange then how about starting with small baby steps.

There's a technique called mirror work that is perfect for helping one come face to face with who they are, literally. It's the first step I took when I decided to change my life. I realized I needed to understand how the world sees me so I could adjust it and make it more of how I wanted the world to see me. So I started spending a lot of time with myself. I used the mirror in the early stages because I wanted to look into my eyes and see who was there. That's when I learned that the person I thought I was didn't show up in the world because he was buried underneath layers of habits, false beliefs and unchecked emotions that only projected what I didn't want.

My body language in the past made me come across as desperate, closed up, and sometimes tense. I am by nature more introverted, but back then, I was relatively quiet and hardly ever made eye contact. When having conversations with people, I would have a very neutral expression. In fact, when I started recording myself whenever I was hanging out with friends, I realized I had my arms and legs crossed a lot of the time, and my tone of voice always seemed a bit too weak and lacking confidence. After walking around my apartment with a mirror for several weeks, I had become more comfortable staring at myself, and I also started picking up on the body language that needed an upgrade.

Many of us tend to associate looking in the mirror or self-care with narcissism, but I can assure you, the real reason self-care and taking time to observe yourself in the mirror is profound and almost spiritual. Using the mirror as a Launchpad to discover yourself can and will help you increase self-compassion, self-love, self-acceptance, and emotional resilience. As you do, it will become easy to extend the same compassion to others. It also helps you become more observant about how your body moves, the facial expressions you make, etc. If you choose to spend the next seven days with a mirror or recording yourself as much as possible, especially when doing mundane things like eating, chilling, talking to someone, you'll learn a lot about how you are showing up in the world. Don't be surprised to find that what you think and what's actually happening are sometimes in conflict. If you don't want to walk around recording yourself, simply get a pocket mirror and put it up where you can see it often. It's a great way to learn more about yourself and your body language. If strong emotions or false beliefs are holding you back, spending time with yourself in front of a mirror can help you uncover these hidden layers and liberate the real you so that the world can see you as you were meant to be seen.

Develop Your Body Language

Once you've spent ample time with yourself and started noticing your body language, you now have the opportunity to change it into whatever you desire. Here are some tips to improve your body language.

• Make sure you're sitting up straight. That is as basic as it gets, yet many of us are completely unaware of our posture. Next time you're in a public place like a restaurant or coffee shop, notice how many people are slouching. If you want to come off more confident, don't slouch. Instead, I want you to sit up straight with an erect yet relaxed spine.

• Soften your gaze and smile more. If like me, you realize your facial expressions need a bit of work, the first shifts I encourage is to learn to laugh more and intentionally look into the eyes of the person in front of you. Start doing this with the mirror. Learn to smile, notice how that makes your face look. Once you feel comfortable with that, extend it to other people during a conversation.

• Minimize distracting movements that make you appear anxious or uncomfortable, such as nail-biting, finger drumming, etc.

• Maintain comfortable and natural eye contact. While I don't want you to come across as weird because of your intense stare, I do encourage you to have as much eye contact as possible. This is probably going to be tough at first because you may not be accustomed to looking people in the eye, so again, start practicing with your mirror. Look yourself in the eye and maintain eye contact. Notice how your eyes change as you say different things to yourself such as "thank you for being awesome" or "I love you" and feel for the natural progression of taking away your direct eye contact and bringing it back. Think of it as a dance between lovers. Sometimes you pull in the person with your eyes, and then you naturally let them go as you stare at something else for a pause. With practice, this will get easier.

• Train your arms and hands to move around with more control as that will help you come across more confident. Instead of throwing them around as you walk, or fidgeting as you communicate to another, use your hands to enhance your posture and demonstrate control. If you're telling a story to someone, use your hands to aid the verbal communication as long as you're sure, the listener will understand what you mean with your body language.

• Mirror the other person. Now that you've invested some time to reflect and see yourself clearly, it's good to intentionally mirror others as they speak. But only if you can do it naturally. When done right, mirroring creates an instant bond. An example of how to mirror someone is when the person leans forward, wait a few minutes, and then naturally lean forward too. If the person nods, do the same. Timing is everything, though. You don't want to instantly react because you'll just come across as a copycat.

What If You Have An RBF?

Some people naturally have what's commonly referred to as resting bitch face (RBF) or bitchy resting face. It's a phenomenon that's got everyone talking, blogging, and debating. While in the last few years science researchers have proven that it's real and tried to explain why some people have it, I know for a fact most people would rather get rid of their RBF. Back in 2016, behavioral researchers with international research and innovation firm Noldus Information Technology by the names Jason Rogers and Abbe Macbeth decided to investigate. They used Noldus's FaceReader (a sophisticated tool engineered) to identify specific expressions based on a catalog of more than 10,000 images of human faces. Their software is able to examine faces via live camera, a photo, video clip, etc. and then gets to work mapping out five hundred points on the human face, after which it can analyze and assign expression based on the eight human emotions that are most basic to us. These are sadness, happiness, anger, fear, surprise, contempt, disgust, and neutral. Rogers and Macbeth established a baseline for this experiment by running a series of genuinely expressionless faces through FaceReader. They realized that a standard benchmark where little to no emotion was expressed on a face is about 3%. So these genuinely blank faces were 3% emotion and 97% neutral. Then they fed the software celebrity faces known to have RBF, and the level of emotion spiked from three to six percent. Macbeth reported that the significant change in percentage came from 'contempt.' They also learned through this experiment that RBF isn't just a female phenomenon. Men can have it in equal measure, although at the moment, we see it more in women.

Celebrities like Victoria Beckham, Kirsten Stewart, and even Kanye West are known for their RBFs. Some people like to own it and unapologetically wear it in the world, while others like my friend Jenny would do anything to get rid of it.

Jenny has suffered bouts of depression since her teen years. I like Jenny, and we grew up in the same neighborhood, went to the same schools, church, neighborhood activities, etc. as far back as I can remember. She's always saying that people usually say something about her face looks unapproachable. She feels like people judge her too much because they think she's judging them. As such, making friends has been an enormous obstacle. Even when I bring her to a party with me, she'll just sit on her own waiting for people to come to her, and by the end of the night, she'll utter something like, "*there's nothing I can do about it. It's not like I can get a new face or something.*" Whether or not this is a learned defense mechanism or people with RBF actually feel contempt is up for debate, and the truth is we can't make a blanket judgment because every human is different. What I can say is if you'd like to make your life a little easier and get along with people more, softening up your RBF is probably a good move. Here's how I encourage you to to start improving your RBF:

• Take up some pranayama toga and do some om chanting. This is not only good for your emotional and spiritual growth, but it's also proven to help exercise those muscles that are needed to eliminate RBF.

• Exercise your head and throat regularly. If you're a fan of musical instruments, now would be an excellent time to pick up wind or rhythmic instruments.

• Pay attention to your eye movement and how you direct your gaze. You might realize they tend to appear more downcast, so when looking at someone, try to look upwards at them.

• Use makeup if you are a woman. Makeup on your eyes, when done correctly, can turn downcast eyes into upcast and more open eyes.

• Engage your cheekbones when smiling. The more you engage your cheekbones intentionally, the more uplifted your entire face will be, which will make you look bright, interested, and awake.

• Practise smiling more. Some of us haven't grown up in an environment that encouraged smiling and joyful energy. Perhaps a very anxious or even abusive parent raised you. That can permanently mess with your facial expression. In such cases, smiling would be quite unnatural, and you would need time, willingness, practice, and a mirror to retrain yourself into frequently holding up a smile. And if you can't work your way up to a smile, at least soften your face muscles and hold your cheeks up to create a softer look.

• Practise forgiveness. If you realize that your RBF is actually hiding contempt, it's time to do something about that. Makeup and fake smiling won't cut it. You need to work on those internal issues. Forgive yourself, let go or the past, and forgive the person or situation because you can't go back and change or prevent what happened. But you can certainly choose to stop carrying that burden. If you have unresolved bitterness, anger, remorse, regret, or any kind of contempt, do yourself a huge favor and let that oppressive past go. Then watch how different and light your body feels.

Don't Let Anything Give You Away.

I once heard of a story about a man who was in the middle of closing the biggest deal of his life. In the middle of the negotiations, he received an emergency call letting him know his wife, who was due to give birth to their first child, had just gone into labor and was being rushed to the hospital. They had been trying to have a baby for years. That was a big moment for him. Emotions were flooding in as he received the call. He was about an hour's drive away from the hospital and still in the middle of a deal that hinged on him. What did he do? Took a deep breath, calmed himself down, wore his poker face, and walked back into the conference room to focus on the deal. No one in that room ever found out what the man was going through, and by the time that meeting was over, he'd sealed a deal that secured his promotion as VP of sales in charge of the entire region. Life is ever-changing and often throws us all kinds of curveballs, some that are positive and some that appear negative. How are we to deal with that?

For most people, any encounter of a situation or news that feels out of their control immediately leads to an outburst of emotion. Everything in their immediate environment gets disrupted. Concentration, calmness, and focus are thrown out the window. If it was something negative, then anger, resentment, yelling, and outrage are expressed. In the case of the above story, it would be nervousness, joy, excitement, etc. which at that moment would still throw the man off his game.

Not only is it our job to deal with our emotions, but we must also get better at controlling the natural impulses and reactions that get triggered when presented with news we weren't prepared for. And I don't just mean the big reactions that can be spotted a mile away. I am also referring to subtle micro-expressions that are often transmitted by the body.

You might have heard this term "poker face" in various settings. It's not just relevant in Las Vegas. Many business leaders are known to be very skillful at having poker faces. It's one of the best-kept secrets that enable successful leaders to mask and control their emotions. Don't be fooled. This isn't a natural skill to develop, but with practice, anyone can get better at staying cool and calm under pressure.

Don't crack under pressure.
Ever noticed how calm and cool Dominic Toretto (the main protagonist in Fast and Furious) is even when everything around him seems to be going to hell? That's probably one of the reasons his audience adores him. To keep that level of control makes you a powerful driver and an even more powerful human being. You want to strive to be the same because whether you realize it or not, you're a leader in your world. So the next time you receive devastating, disappointing, or even nerve-wracking news, don't let anything give you away. Instead, try some of these tactics.

• Relax your facial muscles. The more relaxed your face is, the harder it will be for someone to identify what you are thinking or feeling.

• Pause for 60 seconds. Give yourself a moment just to be with yourself and check-in. Maintain silence for those sixty seconds no matter how badly you want to say something. If you're on the phone, say thank you and hang up then step away for that minute. If it's in person, say thank you and excuse yourself. You need this time to implement the next step.

• Breathe. Take a deep inhale. Exhale slowly. Repeat this deep breathing until you feel your heartbeat slowing down. So many leaders have publicly shared that by deep breathing for a minute or so, they are better able to deal with a situation and think clearly.

• Check your body language and facial expression. Notice what posture you've got. Are you standing erect and confident, or have you drooped? Are your shoulders tense? Fix them. Are your eyes blinking too much? Is your jaw clenched? Have your cheeks turned hot? Notice what's happening on the outside, and allow yourself to be okay with this shift only for a moment. Then work on changing it to become what you want.

• Notice your emotions. If you can name the feelings that are flooding your mind and the sensations that are going on within your body, then do it. Naming something helps to dissipate it. For example, "I feel tightness in my chest" or "my throat feels parched." Make sure, however, that once you name how you're feeling and where you're feeling it, you immediately soothe yourself with the deep breathing and a nice statement. This is where you need to coach or parent yourself. You can comfort yourself with a statement such as, "I'm okay. I'm breathing. I will be fine." You can even go further and give yourself a pep talk. Many leaders secretly give themselves pep talks to calm their nerves, and it works. Create your own pep talk and put it to use whenever these situations arise.

• Access your happy place fast. Is there a picture of a place or a person you can bring to mind in this situation to bring about a sense of joy and security? For me, it's always the beach. As long as I can hold the image in my mind of being in my favorite beach spot for a minute or so, everything will change. For some people, it's a memory of their childhood pet or a favorite vacation spot. Find whatever works for you and hold that single image in your mind until you feel and internal and external shift.

• Work on having more control over your facial expression. Train your face to express calm outwardly no matter what. You can develop the kind of facial expression that only gives away the feeling that "you're in control" regardless of the situation. Sometimes we realize our faces are a bit dysfunctional in that they don't express the happiness and satisfaction that often helps people feel good around us. If that happens to be you, then I encourage you to study your face in the mirror and burn into your brain the kind of look you would like to have at any given moment. Once you've chosen a look that feels right for you, keep working at it until it becomes a default setting or at least easy to put on when you need to reset.

One last thing I want to mention before we move to the more technical aspect of analyzing people is you need to know your telltale signals and tone them down. We all have one or two innate habits that immediately inform others what we are thinking or feeling without ever saying a word. If someone is observant enough and really wants to get under your skin, all they'd have to do is pick up your telltale sign. So, here's a simple action step for you: Find someone you trust and ask them to help you identify a habit or two that usually gives you off. Something you do that makes them know you're either excited or enraged at any given moment. The next time this person spots the sign, have them give you a heads up so you can become aware of yourself in-the-moment. Over time, you will find that becoming more present when those impulsive reactions pop up will enable you to start controlling and even eliminate them from your life.

Chapter 04: Reading Body Movements

You've arrived at the point where we start to get technical and learn the meaning behind body movement so you can start putting to work everything you've learned about reading people. I want to make sure this chapter goes deep enough and addresses all the significant areas of the body that you need to learn to interpret.

The Face

Our face continually transmits information, whether we know it or not. Think of it more like a projector sharing with the world what's going on on the inside. But there are many myths around what a face is saying that you need to become aware of to avoid misinterpretation.

Depending on one's ethnic or cultural background (and at times, it may also be that someone is introverted or extroverted), their facial expression may or may not be easily understood by you. I want you to avoid miscommunication. To do that, you need to look deeper than just commonly promoted ideas. For example, all our faces are coated with numerous creases and lines along with varying degrees of thickness. So that means a person's face is always transmitting some information. But are you able to skillfully figure out what that information is?

Common sense dictates that when a person is relaxed, their facial muscles will also be relaxed. The opposite is also true. And suppose you're speaking with someone who seems to convey a compelling emotional message verbally, yet looking at his or her facial expression, not much intensity is demonstrated. What does that tell you? Perhaps the person isn't as emotionally stimulated as they want you to believe. Of course, the more you know this person and understand their baseline behavior, the easier it can be to notice this difference. The primary emotions we tend to express frequently through our facial expressions include happiness, sadness, anger, surprise, disgust, fear, confusion, excitement, desire, and contempt.

Facial expressions, although a double-edged sword depending on how we use them, makes it easy to read body language. You can spot a happy face, sad face, depressed face, or angry face a mile away. The lesson for you, in this case, isn't about learning to spot and read faces, but instead, it's about giving digging deeper to uncover some of the hidden messages that often go unnoticed. Many people have learned to mask their emotions. They might be "faking a smile" or pretending to be interested in you. In such cases, you need to know how to detect their microexpressions. Whenever someone is showing an expression that contradicts what they are feeling inside, you will catch a glimpse of their real expression in an instant as they attempt to control their body language. Usually, these facial expressions only last a split second, and although hard to catch, it's good to start looking out for them whenever you interact with someone.

Eyes And Eyebrows

We often hear the eyes are the windows to the soul. But how much of the information around reading eye movement is accurately representative of the truth? There are a lot of myths around the eyes that we need to address first. For a long time, it was believed that an honest person always looks you in the eye, and so when someone doesn't, it was considered a sign of deception. That is one of the many myths you need to become aware of. As we mentioned in a previous chapter, every culture carries its own tradition around how much eye contact is acceptable. So if you're talking to someone and they don't start you straight in the eye, don't be so quick to judge. Instead of getting biased, use these standard signals to try and pick up what the person is communicating.

Notice The Pupil.

When someone is excited about something, the natural reaction of the pupil is to dilate. The opposite is also true. If the person is angry or offended for some reason, the pupil will automatically contract. Taking notice of the size of the pupil and the different changes that occur as you interact with them can help you get a sense of how the other person is receiving the communication and whether or not you are keeping their attention.

The Eyebrows

Aside from the eyes and the pupil, your eyebrows or that of a counterpart also expresses feelings. For example, in women, raised eyebrows are indicative of friendless and sometimes even submissiveness. With the overabundance of selfies on social media today, I encourage you to find selfies of people who are showing off their faces. Notice that you'll tend to feel more attractive to a particular "look," and more often than not, if you dig deep, it will have a lot to do with the eyes and the eyebrows. Raised eyebrows and lowered eyelids come across as very attractive and suggestive. It's not threatening. But lowered eyebrows give off a mean authoritative look. They tend to communicate dominance and aggression. Combine lowered eyebrows with glaring eyes, and no one will want to hang around you!

How To Read People Using The Eyes:

The first step is to figure out someone's baseline. Everyone will have their baseline, i.e., how they act under normal, non-threatening conditions. That means you need to invest some time with the person you want to read and casually engage in neutral topics that they would have no reason to get defensive or lie about. Daily mundane things like the weather are a great starting point. Once you understand the baseline, it's easy to spot the clues that let you know something is off. Some of these clues include:

Squinting - this often occurs when someone doesn't like you or what you're saying. It can indicate suspicion unless it's a dimly lit environment in which case they might be attempting to see more clearly. If someone squints at you, take a moment to address him or her directly and clarify your statement.

Eye blocking - this often occurs in the form of covering or shielding. You can also see a lot of blinking or eye rubbing. It's a powerful display of disagreement, disbelief, or fear.

Eye direction - several studies say when someone looks up to the right, they are lying or tapping into their imagination. When they look up to the left, they are remembering something by tapping into the memory of the brain. Vanessa Van Edwards, from the science of people, shares a simple formula that anyone can follow.

Looking to their right is Auditory Thought (e.g., remembering a song).

Looking to their left is visual Thought (e.g., remembering the color of a dress).

Looking down to their right is someone creating a feeling or sensory memory (e.g., thinking what it would be like to swim in jello).

Looking down to their left is someone talking to himself or herself. [Source: scienceofpeople.com]

Mouth

Does the mouth also communicate important information? Absolutely. The mouth, especially the way the lips are positioned and used, can help us understand a lot about what someone else feels. There are numerous ways to squeeze the lips together, which creates a variety of communication signals. Although men and women use their lips to communicate non-verbally, you might realize, most of the time, that women will express far more with their mouths than men.

Lips are actually part of our skin. They are thin, sensitive, and packed with a lot of necessary nerve endings that make them very useful in our human interactions. If you noticed, other animals tend to have very different lips than ours. We seem to have extremely versatile and attractive lips, which is probably why they play a huge role in our sexual communication.

For example, when it comes to the emotional act of kissing, aren't you glad you've got lips that help you learn a lot about your partner just from a kiss? Unconsciously you can tell a lot from a kiss, and that's a key example of non-verbal communication. But whether you're kissing a lover or not, there are other cues you can look for when reading someone's mouth and lips. Some of these signals will come in very handy the next time you're engaged in conversation with a woman, as they tend to use many of these cues to communicate.

Perking the lips - This is usually a playful and cute gesture often communicated between lovers. Either to blow a kiss or to come across as flirtatious, so if you're planning on using it, make sure it's the right moment and the right person.

Pouting - This is when the lower lip slid forward. Often used to indicate displeasure and insult.

Licking the lips - This can vary depending on the context, so make sure you understand what's happening to avoid misinterpretation. If it's a sexual lick, then it will be an intentional gesture that starts in the corner of the mouth, licking the upper lip and then the lower in a slow sensual motion. It's indicative of desire. The other kind of lick is the nervous lick, which is quick and partial, often characteristic of tension. People who self-lick are often trying to release some pressure by self-soothing.

When you see someone biting their lip nervously, you can assume it means they are uncomfortable or uncertain about something. Unless, of course, they are trying to moisten their chapped lips or if it's a habit developed when they are in deep concentration.

Biting the lips - similar to licking it is also used to either communicate sexual desire, especially when a person wants to appear sexy. But it can also be a form of self-restraint, meaning the person is trying to contain anger or hold back thoughts.

The main thing to remember with all lip communication is that it is often indicative of sexual communication and tension control. We tend to either touch or use them for stimulation or self-comfort.

Breathing

How deep, shallow quick, or slow the breath of a person is as they interact with you can tell you a lot about them. Breathing and emotions are connected, and a skillful person can easily read feelings through observing how another is breathing. Here are some signals to help you learn to determine what breathing patterns mean.

Heavy rapid breathing:
This might be an indication of fatigue and/or fear. When the heart beats faster, and the lungs need more oxygen, the breath becomes heavy and rapid. It feels like you need to catch your breath. Whenever you notice someone displaying that "catch your breath" type of scenario, it could be that they are tired from physical exertion, or they are terrified of something.

Deep breath:
That may be an indication of love or attraction and excitement, which is an intense positive emotion, or it could be anger and fear, which are also very intense on the negative side of the spectrum. Deep breathing is easy to notice if you're observant. If you give someone some news and they hold their breath or they take a deep breath in just before yelling out, that person is going to go through deep breathing patterns. On the other hand, we can spot this deep breathing when a guy wants to impress a girl. Before walking up to her, he might take a deep breath in to make his upper body look broader, and his abs look smaller, which is often attractive to the opposite sex.

Sigh:
Sighs generally communicate hopelessness, sadness, but sometimes they can be used to convey relief. If someone is waiting on a long struggle to end, they might sigh to express their sense of tiredness while hoping and praying for that relief to come.

Arms, Hands, And Fingers.

Now let's talk about different arm positions and what they might indicate.

The most basic and natural arms and hands gesture you will see is hands rested tot the sides of the body.

Hands behind the back can be a signal of comfort and authority, or it can be the opposite i.e., tension and anxiety. How can you tell which is which? Observe for a while how the hands are wrapped around each other. If one hand is held easy in the palm of the other behind the back, that is more likely a superior position. In such a situation, the person would be seeking to use his body to demonstrate that he is secure and dominant in that particular context. Think of an army instructor or a professor on a podium. Suppose the person suddenly feels threatened by something or someone, they are more likely to shift into a tightly clenched grip to help them "keep it together" and if it becomes too much, they might change into a different position like folded arms.

Hands in the pockets tend to be received as something only people who are embarrassed or people who are hiding something (like the bad habit of fidgeting or nail biting) do.

Legs and Feet

Not many people pay attention to what the legs and feet are communicating in their own bodies as well as those of others. I mean, when was the last time you consciously monitored where your feet pointed as you engaged in conversation with another?

The reason we tend to neglect our legs and feet is that they are, in fact, furthest away from the brain, which prefers to focus on the face since that's the area of our body that's usually in the spotlight. But if you want to become great at reading people and their intention, paying closer attention to the legs and feet is a must. Take some time to notice what you do with your legs with you're standing as well as when you're sitting. What about the direction of your feet? Where do they point when having a business interaction? Does it change when you have a social or intimate interaction? How stable are you when standing?

Experts report there is a correlation between how a person stands and his or her self-confidence. For example, introverts will tend to stand with both feet very close to each other. This is usually a symbol of submission, and it makes the person a smaller target. It's easy to topple over someone standing like that both physically and socially. So if you're the kind of person who doesn't like drawing attention, it's likely your stance will be very narrow.

In contrast, if you're confident and want to come across as strong and dominating, your stance will be wider. When it comes to the direction of the feet, planting both feet directly in front of someone can come across as intimidating and hostile unless it's a person you're sexually attracted to, and you want to pass on that you're intimately interested in that person. For a more relaxed position, consider standing with your weight on one foot while the other points to the side. Now let's talk about some of the meanings you might derive when you spot different leg positions.

The stork is a very female gesture where she will stand on one foot while tucking the other behind her around the calf region (to form a stork). Females use this a defense mechanism more than males mainly because men just lack that level of flexibility. It's so easy to destabilize such an individual, though, and perhaps above all else, when you notice this in a girl, be mindful of your approach because often this stance is communicating timidity and fear. Be gentle and attentive with your approach in the same way as you would a frightened animal.

Crossed legs, which is very common, doesn't necessarily mean the person is closed-minded. That's just a myth. It all depends on the context. For example, a person might want to pee. Or they might be relaxed in that environment in which case they are communicating that they are currently tied up and engaged in the ongoing interaction. The only time it can be a negative sign is where there's an outcome of suspicion, and the person is reserved and unwilling to change their mind. If they are just not convinced by you, they might cross their legs.

Happy feet are easy to spot and are often a result of feeling excited. If you want to tell a boy or girl who is walking on cloud nine, you just have to observe how "springy" their steps are. Happy people walk with jumpy strides; it's like they are about to lift off from the ground.

Chapter 05: Seeing Body Language as a Whole

Aside from the specific gestures and particular body movements, you also want to start creating a baseline that helps you analyze the cues the body is communicating as a whole. There's always a general non-verbal communication being transmitted when you observe a person. For example, you might notice how animated, edgy, calm, poised, or stoic the person in front of you might appear. He or she might be expressing a sense of vibrant energy and seem very upbeat and happy, or they might be cumbersome and dull. In this chapter, we want to address some of the more prominent body movements and what they indicate to help you read people more accurately.

The Chest:

• Chest protrusion can be considered a sexual or aggressive body language posture. Men do it to appear more dominant, which is meant to repel other aggressive men and attract members of the opposite sex. When women do it, they usually want to draw attention to their breasts, making them appear large so they can attract the attention of men.

• Chest puffing occurs when a person inhales deeply and expands the lungs, so they appear larger and more dominant. Mostly a very male body posture. You can read this as a sign of conflict arising. Often when a guy does this, he also arches his back and holds his head up in an exaggerated form to amplify the puffed up chest.

The Shoulder:

• Shoulder embrace usually occurs between adult men or between mother and her child and is generally non-sexual in nature. Read it as a non-verbal sign of affection where the arms are put around another's shoulder.

• Shoulder shrugs or a shoulder rise is usually an expression of uncertainty or doubt. You can read it as a sign of indifference, resignation, helplessness, or even ignorance depending on the context. The person will move his or her shoulders upward toward the ears.

The Hips

• The hip tilt is a female move. A woman will slouch to one side forcing her hips to emphasize her curves. It's a simple way of drawing attention to her genitals. In the fashion world, you see it a lot, and perhaps the more exaggerated version known as the catwalk all meant to draw the eye to the beaconing genital region.

• Hip embrace is when two people (usual lovers) walk side by side with their arms around the hips of the other. Read it as a sharp display of intimacy.

The Torso

• Torso shield is when a person uses their arm or an object to shield their chest area to protect it from a perceived threat. This can be subtle in the form of holding a drink across the body, playing with their tie or cufflink, or it can be more obvious like a full arm cross. Read it as an expression that the other person is protecting himself or herself from something, and they have a difference of opinion.

• Torso splay is a dominant body posture in which the person lies back in a comfortable position with the chest puffed out and open, almost challenging an attack. Read it as a sign of high comfort and the person communicating to you that they feel in charge of the situation.

Expressing Yourself With Body Posture

Did you know that you express yourself daily using your body posture? Posture is the way you hold your body during movement and while at rest. There are two main types of body posture that you need to become aware of. Dynamic and static body posture. Let's take a closer look at each.

Dynamic Posture

It refers to how the body is aligned during activity or movement. Generally, this involves moving the whole body in a particular way. With dynamic posture, we want to make sure we move lightly, and the knees are slightly bent, the senses and mind are engaged, etc. Movement such as walking, running, jumping, dancing, and so on are all forms of dynamic posture. Our bodies are highly adaptable, and they are ever looking for the path of least resistance, which is why poor posture is terrible because it inevitably becomes the default setting, which eventually leads to decreased flexibility, performance, and lots of unnecessary aches.

Static Posture

Static posture refers to how your body is aligned when stationary or when standing. Spend the next week observing how you stand. Keep a mirror in all the rooms where you frequently stand so you can see yourself. Are your shoulders rounded, level, or elevated? What about your head? Do your knees track over the second and third toes? You want to make sure your body can hold itself up with the least amount of energy yet maintaining proper form.

The key to good posture, whether it is dynamic or static, is the position of your spine. There are three natural curves you want to become more familiar with: the neck, the mid-back, and the low back curve. Good posture is about maintaining these curves, not increasing or decreasing them. How can you do this? Make sure your head is always above your shoulders, and the top of your shoulder is over your hips. In our modern society, give the fact that we spent so much time sitting behind a desk or typing on a computer, you need to keep doing some check-ins throughout the day to ensure you're maintaining good posture. If you carry around heavy bags or lift heavy things often, then you also need to keep reinforcing the right alignment because these activities often through off our alignment.

Did You Know Your Posture Could Affect Your Health?

Experts tell us that slouching can wear out your spine, making it more fragile and prone to injury. It can also lead to back pain, shoulder pain, decrease your flexibility, affect your balance, make it harder for you to breathe and digest your food, etc. So you want to do everything possible to ensure you're maintaining good dynamic and static posture. For starters, exercise, and stretch more often. Take up some yoga and tai chi, as they are known to help with body awareness. It's also important to elevate your work surface area, especially if you're using a computer. Make sure it's a comfortable height. I also encourage you to stretch your muscles often as this helps relieve your muscle tension and switch positions often, especially when sitting. If you notice your standing posture needs a little help, then I encourage you to keep your shoulders back and head level.

Pull your stomach in as if you want your navel to touch your spine and keep your feet about shoulder-width apart. With practice, you'll notice it gets easier to keep your arms naturally at your side and have most of your weight on the balls of your feet. That will automatically lead to you looking and feeling good.

Aside from gaining this vital knowledge of your body posture and how it affects your physical appearance as well as your health, posture is also essential for transmitting non-verbal cues.

The 2 Forms Of Non-Verbal Posture

When reading body language, either your own or another person's, the two primary signals you might receive are open or closed. Open means the person is not defensive and is more willing and open to interacting. The closed posture means the opposite, of course. To a certain degree, the posture form you read in a person can tell you how confident they are and how receptive they are likely to be if you interacted. For example, imagine walking up to two strangers, both sitting at a table because you needed directions to the bathroom. One had their arms crossed, and he was hunched over while the other sat with an open chest, head level, shoulders, and faced relaxed. Who would you talk to first?

Anytime you interact with someone or if you're about to interact with a person, take a moment to read the form they have. They will either be transmitting a closed or open posture.

- Closed Posture - whether the trunk of the body is left open and exposed. That usually indicates the person is very open to interacting and friendly.
- Open Posture - where the trunk of the body is hidden in the form of crossing arms and legs or hunching forward. That usually means the person is not that friendly, is not willing to engage, and might be anxious or even hostile.

Notice how much easier it feels to walk up and interact with people who carry themselves in an open posture. Most of the "cool guys" tend to carry themselves in a way that makes them look "open" like you need to be around them. Observe how many people around you, especially the ones you like are communicating this form of posture. Even when you want to approach someone you feel attracted to, it will be more comforting, and you'll have more confidence when the person looks open instead of closed. Now that you have this awareness, pay more attention to the form of non-verbal posture, you transmit when interacting with others in social settings.

How Far Should We Be?

I struggle with this one because I know cultures are different, and individuals are different. In the Latin culture, for example, they can get up close and personal when talking to you, which for an American is simply absurd. We tend to like our personal space. Some of us even more than others. Doesn't it suck when someone gets too close to your face?

Since there cannot be any rigid rules around this topic because "personal space" varies from one person to the next, I encourage you to experiment based on your personal preference. In other words, stick to the one golden rule I have. Treat others, as you would like to be treated. If, like me, you enjoy a lot of personal space, make sure you are always giving that same space to the people you interact with. It would also help to be more present and mindful in your conversations and pay attention to the body language such as the direction of the feet and the hips as well as the general sway or body movement the person makes if you happen to be standing. Suppose you're speaking to a girl, and you notice she keeps rocking subtly back and forth, taking a step back. Clearly, she likes a little space. Give it to her. If you notice someone is moving closer and closer to you, then they probably don't mind reducing the distance between the two of you. Other simple things you can do to ensure you're not making anyone uncomfortable is to do your best to stand at a distance where you can't accidentally touch or hit someone as you move your hands. It's often a good estimate and creates enough distance to read the other person's preference. If you walk into a theatre or auditorium and it isn't crowded, get into the habit of leaving an extra seat between you and the next person. You also want to avoid leaning over someone's shoulder if you're not really close. If you're working in an office, set clear boundaries, and observe the cues that others give of their personal boundaries. At least 4 feet away when you're not certain should give you a safe distance and help you communicate that you respect personal space.

Listening Closely

Developing the ability to listen actively, as I mentioned in an earlier chapter, is part of the skill of reading and analyzing people effectively. There's much to learn from a person's tone. It's not so much what they say but how they say it and the unspoken cues they send out. Think about it; everyone you know has a unique way of expressing himself or herself. Even if you pronounce the same word, no two people can say it exactly the same way. How we express ourselves is as unique as our fingerprints. Some people say something, and it comes across as pushy. Others say it, and it comes across as nasty while others can literally insult you, yet you never realize it till much later. Again, I want you to remember that as you listen attentively to what someone is saying, the best way to get the full message is to pay attention to the tonality of their voice (i.e., is it confident, shrieking, etc.), the words they choose to use and how they say it. Many experts have conducted thorough research that proves the tone we use can shut down communication, trust, confidence, agreement, and possibilities. That's why I encourage you to focus on how you say things.

When you want to really understand the hidden cues someone is sending, learn to pick up on non-verbal qualities such as the pitch, voice quality, amplitude, rate, as well as the pauses and hesitations between words. If you pay close attention, you can be able to quickly decipher whether the person is truly sincere with their warmth, concern, enthusiasm, and confidence or whether they're faking it. Even if the person is trying hard to play it cool, something will give it away.

For example, have you ever experienced meeting a friend that you know pretty well who just seemed off? Their energy seemed dense, and you could tell they were troubled by something. Yet all they did was slap on this wide fake smile, tell you how good life was, etc. They were trying really hard to put on that mask of positivity and happiness, but you just knew they were dealing with something.

Many of us can even spot a depressed or resentful person 90 seconds after we initiate conversation. Unfortunately, it happens mostly unconsciously, so we rarely recognize it as "depression" or "resentment." Often we just feel repelled by the other person and want to avid their presence. Unless, of course, we are in the same emotional state. Then we feel the strong resonance. Either way, the more closely you listen to what and how someone speaks and utilizes their tone, the more you will read their body language effectively.

If you want to improve your body posture and tone of voice, consider the following:
1. Smile more.
2. Use more pauses as you speak, especially when you want to emphasize something.
3. Practice speaking at a lower pitch when you want to convey more credibility.
4. Whenever possible, especially during face-to-face conversations, try to synchronize your tone of voice to match that of your conversational partner.

Chapter 06: Positive Versus Negative

At this point in the book, you are well versed in the non-verbal language of the body. It's now time to dive into the details that often go unnoticed yet impact results nonetheless. During your interactions, whether personal or professional, a lot of communication is taking place with or without words. Your face and body are transmitting hundreds of thousands of signals, and you are in a position to read and analyze the transmission your counterpart is sending to you. The overall theme of this communication can be negative or positive. Sometimes it can be conflicting, which usually creates mixed signals and leaves the receiving party feeling confused and unsure about you. Because we want to make you masterful at this art of reading people, you must take control of the transmission you send out because a negative one will often alienate others and hurt your objectives even without you knowing.

How Often Do You Show Positive And Negative Body Language?

There's nothing wrong with showing negative body language if you are intentionally looking to convey that message. If you're angry and want people to know they've hurt you, then it's perfectly fine to hold a negative posture. The problem occurs when you want to be likable or influence another, yet your body language conveys the opposite of what you'd like. For example, I want you to imagine having the opportunity to interview with the owner of a company you dream of working for. As you walk up to the reception area and the owner's assistance directs you toward the office where your potential new boss eagerly awaits you, all you can think about is how much you want to impress him. Right?

Now I want you to imagine what would happen if you walked into the meeting with your resume, appropriately dressed, and ready to impress. Unfortunately, some of your unconscious habits might kick in due to your nervousness and cause you to act and convey non-verbal signals that completely repel your new boss. By the time you walk out of his office, you feel deflated because you could tell things weren't going your way, and you have no idea what you did wrong. It's easy to come to irrational conclusions like "he doesn't get you" or "he didn't give you enough of a chance" or so many other reasonably sounding excuses. The fact remains; your communication fell flat and harmed your ability to sell the man into hiring you. Most of the time, the big screw up happens with the non-verbal cues. See what I mean? By the end of this chapter, you will know how to keep those non-verbal signals in check so that you can avoid losing or messing up something you care about.

Negative Body Language

What is negative body language?

A negative body language is, in essence, the opposite of a positive body language, which we'll talk about in a bit. It's a way of expressing yourself non-verbally that makes you come across as closed and unapproachable. It's defensive and repels people.

You come across as unfriendly, perhaps even hostile or a possible threat. It can also be expressed as lack of interest, too much dominance or submission, or any other negatively coated extreme.

Negative body language can harm all your relationships and create a lot of misunderstandings. Let's go over some of the negative body language signals you want to look out for and improve in your own life.

• Closed off body language - is first on this list because it is extremely harmful when you're trying to build rapport with someone. Whether professionally or in an intimate setting, if you come across as unapproachable and if you carry yourself in the closed body posture, it will create a wall and prevent you from getting what you want in life. Take notice of yourself when in a meeting or a social gathering. How are you responding to people? Are you engaged with others in conversation? Is your body standoffish to other people?

• Slumping - is something many interviewees do unconsciously. No wonder they never get hired. A slumped posture shows a lack of confidence and energy. It comes across as laziness or weakness. No business professional in their right mind will hire an employee who is already communicating that they lack energy and confidence. Hunching over or slumping always sends a wrong signal, whether you're trying to impress a girl or a potential employer. So take notice of how you have been carrying yourself, especially during important meetings.

• The wrong handshake - helps us form the first impression of a new person. If you can recall in an earlier chapter where I shared the experiment carried out by Vincent, his first impression was different when we went from a weak handshake to the right handshake. What handshake do you give? A wrong handshake is one that is either too weak or too strong. What you need is a happy medium that preferably engages both arms as you handshake a person.

• Scrunched-up face - is usually very off-putting, and some of us do it unintentionally. If someone is talking to you and you unconsciously furrow your eyebrows and scrunch up your face, they will naturally pick up that being around you isn't the best idea. Such an expression tends to come across as hostile. Instead, you want to come across as interested and friendly.

• The submissive handshake - is when your palm is facing up and falls underneath the palm of the other person during a handshake. It makes you look submissive. I didn't consciously realize it, but for a long time, I would frequently use this type of handshake and send off the wrong vibes.

• The wet fish handshake - is probably one of the worst ones in the world. It sends a negative signal to the person shaking your hand and is interpreted as that of a weak and uncommitted character. If your hands tend to get cold and sweaty, work on improving that because it will always send off the wrong signals.

• The fingertip handshake - is another type of handshake you need to avoid. It's usually when two people barely touch the fingertips of each other. If they do touch, it's a very light stroke as if they are being forced to shake hands. The handshake signals a lack of confidence and self-esteem. Remember, my smart friend, who failed to land his dream job back in college? This was one of his downfalls. In tracing back his missteps, he realized the first thing the interviewer did before starting the meeting was to shake his hand. And we always made fun of his wimpy handshake. He did realize how much that weak handshake would cost him until after he repelled someone he really wanted to impress.

Okay, now that you have an idea of the negative body language and postures, let's talk about the positive.

Positive Body Language

What is positive body language?
A positive body language is a way of non-verbally expressing yourself that makes you come across as likable, receptive, trustworthy, and upbeat. It puts you in a position of comfort, dignity, and friendliness with others. You come across as open and approachable.

With a positive comes the show of confidence and assertiveness, which is good. You want to be able to clearly communicate your opinion without offending anyone. Having a positive body language will help you become successful in your personal and professional relationships. It can help you convey respect amongst your peers, and it also causes people to naturally respect and want to follow your advice and leadership. Since many of our conversations take place while we are in standing position, here are some excellent rules of the game to apply to your life. I also encourage you to start taking notice of the people you interact with and how they hold themselves while you carry out the conversation.

• Always stand with an erect spine. Make sure your back is straight, and head leveled out, as this will give the impression of being tall. It will also ensure you avoid the negative body posture of slumping that I just mentioned.

• Free your hands. Some men like to pocket their hands while interacting with others. This posture tends to indicate a lack of respect and disinterest, so avoid it as much as possible. Keep your hands out, and open resting on the side in a relaxed manner is you want to come across as friendly and approachable.

If you're in a cocktail party and you're holding a drink, then be mindful that you don't cover your chest area with the drink.

• Face the person. That means whenever the situation is appropriate, you want to be facing the person that you're in communication with. It will also allow you to read the body language of the other person effortlessly. To do this properly, create an imaginary line between your heart and the other person's heart.

If you notice the other person is perhaps standing sideways or the hips and feet are pointing away from you, then I encourage you to terminate that conversation quickly as that is usually an indication that they can't wait to get rid of you. One more thing to note is the position of your hands. Consider placing your hands over your waist or standing akimbo but never cross your arms as that might come off as a negative body signal.

• Move your limbs a little. I don't encourage you to stand still like a rock because I think a more natural body language movement always includes a little sway, some hands, and legs motion, etc. Moving your hands in the right way can help emphasize that you are interested and engaged in that conversation. Just be mindful of the gestures and also what you're doing with those hands and fingers. Also, remember to keep your legs hip-width apart and your palms open as much as feels comfortable to you.

• Use the politician's handshake. It is considered one of the most powerful handshakes in the world and, when done right, conveys sincerity and trust. It can quickly establish a bond between two people, no wonder the politicians use it a lot. To do it right, you need to engage both your hands. Make sure you place one hand in the palm-up position and then apply your second hand lightly on top of the back of the palm of your counterpart.

• Maintain eye contact. Without being creepy, of course. Find a balance between looking the person in the eye and looking away to create a harmonious dance between the two of you. Stare at them too long, and you might send off the wrong signals. Look away too much, and they might think you're not interested.

Remember to look for these signals in the person you're interacting with as well.

When it comes to interacting with others while in a seated position, many of the same concepts shared will apply, for example, always sit with your spine erect and head level to avoid hunching over. If appropriate, leaning slightly toward the person (especially if it's someone you are very familiar with) can help you come across more open and engaged. But don't lean too much as that will compromise your posture. Movement of your hands and legs also matters. With your legs, make sure they are appropriately positioned, depending on the context. If you're in a formal setting, crossing your legs might not be the best idea because sitting with uncrossed legs tends to signify openness and acceptance. Try to give yourself enough legroom to show that you are confident and in charge of yourself. Don't tap with your feet as some people do because most people find it very annoying. I also encourage you to monitor what you do with your hands because massaging yourself or fidgeting comes across as uneasiness and lack of esteem.

Chapter 07: Liar, Liar, Pants On Fire

Lying is something many of us are familiar with. Whether it's little white lies or huge lies that cause devastation, we've all participated in this addictive habit. Believe it or not, a lot of research has been conducted on this topic, and many researchers even report that, in some cases, our need to lie stems from a good place. But more on that in just a bit.

For the most part, as we grow up, many of us try never to make lying a habit, but others simply cannot stop themselves if they wanted to. Those are the kind of people we need to protect ourselves from. Frequently, narcissists fall into the cycle of lying and manipulating others just to get their way. It then becomes beneficial for us to detect when we are in the presence of such a person. Hopefully, everything you have learned so far will make you better at reading the real person behind the mask of personality. In the next chapter, we are going to focus on some of the signals you need to start looking out for whenever you interact with people as well as what the messages mean. But I feel it wouldn't be fair to you if we jumped to that part before discussing the all-important topic of how to spot a liar. That is what this chapter is about.

Why Do We Lie? Is It Always Intentional?

The concept of lying is not binary, and yes, there is always intention behind the lies we tell. To ask whether lying is intentional or not is a low-quality question which will not help you get better at analyzing people and spotting malicious individuals. The fact of the matter is we all lie at some point in our lives. A better question to ask is - what is the intention behind the lie?

The experts studying this subject report that we learn to lie at a very young age. It is, in fact, a developmental milestone, according to modern psychology. At first, we learn what's called antisocial lying or black lies, which is basically lies we tell for personal gain. Most children can and will lie to avoid punishment or chores. As we grow, we start to tell prosocial lies, which are falsehoods told for someone else's benefit. For example, remember that time when a parent encouraged you to express delight or excitement over a sweater or gift from an aunt or uncle that you didn't fancy at all? Or that time when you were forced to pretend the neighbor's pie tasted good just because it's the right thing to do? Prosocial lying is something we generally learn as we are growing, and it is rooted in the need to alleviate suffering or protect someone else from disappointing or hurtful news. A lot of research has been done on developing children to determine whether all lying is wrong and why we do it.

The fact of the matter is that lying is prevalent in our society from as early as three years old. However, it must be firmly noted here that not all lies are made equal. After much research, psychologists and other experts have been able to prove that, in fact, there are three main categories of lies, and they affect the brain's activity in different ways. The first type that most young kids learn very early on is black lies, which, as we said, is very self-serving. The brain's activity on this type of lying shows the amygdala shifting in ways that indicate our bodies and brains don't particularly like this type of behavior. It also increases in frequency in the sense that the more one lies, the more frequently they will continue to lie.

The second type of lying is known as the blue lie, which involves telling an altruistic lie to protect a group they belong to like classmates or family members. An example of this would be a sibling lying to cover up a crime committed by their brother or sister. The blue lie is more complex and develops gradually as the child advances through adolescence into adulthood. Then there are the white lies, also known as prosocial lies, which involve sparing someone pain or suffering. A research team led by Neil Garrett at Princeton University carried out this experiment, which led to the conclusion that not all lies are the same. Some of the lies we learn to tell help bind our families and friends together. They create feelings of trust. Other types of lies destroy these bonds. So it's really not a black and white discussion when it comes to asking why we lie. We also cannot give a blanket answer and suggest that all lying is evil. So how do we go about resolving this?

Well, as far as my personal research has taken me, I can encourage you to categorize the lies. Black lies are obviously not the same as prosocial lies and shouldn't be treated equally. And the best way to make sure you're staying on the right path when it comes to this topic is to remain grounded in the principle that empathy and kindness should be the leading guide. So if the intention is to show you empathy and kindness, the supposed lie was intended for good, and the person might be trying to build a stronger bond with you or show you that he or she cares. If it was self-serving, that indeed that is someone you need to protect yourself from.

Always begin with the question - what was the intention here?

7 Ways To Spot A Liar

If you really want to get good at analyzing people and spotting a liar, you need to commit to observing the people you interact with. While I am going to share some telltale signals that almost every liar unconsciously uses, the fact of the matter is that you can only really confirm that someone is lying if you know them well enough to figure our their baseline communication. What do I mean by this? You need to know how the person usually behaves under normal conditions when they are comfortable and at ease. Only then can you read them effectively. So devote some time to studying and observing the people around you that you want to understand better. Now, onto the seven signals, I promised to share with you that should raise a red flag if someone you're having a conversation with impulsively communicates, especially during an important interaction.

#1. A sudden change of volume or pitch in their voice. When people get nervous, the muscles in the vocal cord might tighten due to increased stress. Sometimes you might even hear the clearing of the throat, which could be an indication of dishonesty.

#2. Increased perspiration, especially around the forehead, chin, or upper lip. That happens because the autonomic nervous system is triggered internally and starts working overtime.

#3. An intense stare or gaze to forcibly maintain eye contact with you can be a signal that the person is lying. That is usually to stimulate a sense of intimidation or control. On the other hand, it might be that the person looks away at critical moments during your conversation, or you notice their blinking rate increasing tremendously.

#4. Too much repetition of words of stammering out of nowhere can be a sign that the person is attempting to buy time as he or she thinks of what to say next. At this point, you should also notice a shift in their tone of voice and speech.

#5. Fidgeting and itching can indicate dishonesty, especially if it also includes rocking of the body back and forth or tapping of the feet. Pay attention to the feet because they can tell you a lot. The more nervous someone feels, the easier it is for these habits to surface to their level, even without conscious awareness. The nervous system also tends to tingle and generate bodily sensations, which can be easily observed if you pay close attention.

#6. Covering the mouth or eyes is a natural tendency when someone is trying to cover up a lie. Take notice of where the hands move to as you ask critical questions or during the length of the conversation. If the person shields his or her eyes of the mouth while responding, it could be an indication of deception.

#7. Grooming gestures are often used by liars to cover up their dishonesty. For women, that can be easily spotted through an impulsive act of straightening her skirt or moving a few strands of hair behind her ear. A man might adjust his shirt cuffs or glasses or maybe his tie. If you're in the middle of a conversation whereby you ask a critical question and all of a sudden, the person starts tidying up the surrounding, that can be a sign of deceit. Ever been in that situation where you say something, and suddenly the pencil isn't in the right place, or the coffee cup is too close and must be moved? Pay attention to such moments as the person could be conveying a non-verbal cue that they are about to deceive you.

Identifying The Kind Of Liar You Are Facing

It's essential to recognize at this point that lying is a very complex topic. Add to that the fact that lying is woven into the fabric of our global culture, and you can be sure there's no getting away from the truth - lying is part of your everyday experience. You just never realized it. Sometimes you are a willing participant in the deception for a variety of reasons (which is why you let it slide), and other times you are not willing to participate. Those are the times you become hurt and against the act of lying. But I can assure you, most of the time you don't even realize you've just been deceived. Experts say that ordinary people can spot liars a little over fifty percent of the time. Shall we increase those odds for a bit more?

One of the things we know about liars is they will often use speech in a particular way. They will use certain words, e.g., "I did not do that" instead of "I didn't do that." Studies show that people who are determined to deny or lie about something will often resort to formal instead of informal language. Liars also like distancing themselves from the subject matter using language as their tool. But it doesn't end there. There's a lot more to this than speech. Body language and attitude are the key ways to help identify a liar. You want to be able to figure out what kind of a liar you're dealing with as early as possible in the interaction. To help you quickly identify what type of liar you're dealing with, here are some basic things you should do.

• Start by asking neutral questions, especially if it's someone you don't know very well. This will enable you to determine their baseline and how they communicate under non-threatening situations. If it's someone you know or have been observing long enough, then you should already have baseline knowledge of how they respond when they are truthful.

• The next thing you want to do is move them into the "hot spot" where you suspect the deception might begin, and as you do, pay close attention to any shift in energy, body language, etc.

• Carefully observe their body language and look for any red flags. Understand that red flags do not mean anything in and of themselves. Someone increasing their blinking rate, shoulder shrugging, fidgeting, adjusting their tie, or shirt cuffs doesn't necessarily indicate deception. But if you notice a cluster of these red flags together as the intensity of the conversation increases, then that is cause for alarm.

• Identify the changes in their facial expressions. More importantly, you're looking for micro-facial expressions. Did something leak for a moment while they were talking? Did you see a glint of contempt or anger just for a split of a second? Did they bite their lip, turn a little pale or begin to sweat on their forehead even though temperatures are cool? Each of these changes signifies an increase in brain activity and could indicate deception is ongoing.

• Listen carefully to the speech pattern and the sentence structure. Liars usually change the tone of their voice when deceiving someone. They might go higher or lower in pitch. They also tend to use over complicate the information being passed on and use words they would typically not use in an attempt to convince you of their lie.

•Psychological distancing is also common for many liars though not all. If the person is distancing themselves from the subject and referring to people as strangers (e.g., that man instead of my neighbor), it's usually an indicator of falsehood.

Realize that human beings are also unique, so there's no accurate lie detector yet, as some people may use behavior that isn't associated with lysing. The better and more professional the liar, the harder it will be to spot them. So even though you now understand how to identify a liar, let's prepare you even more by sharing with you the different types of liars you will have to learn to read. Not all liars are the same. Some are easy to spot, while others require a lot of practice and additional insight, which I will provide in the next chapter. There are five different types of liars that you need to be able to identify. Some more dangerous than others and must be avoided at all costs.

#1. White Liars.

This would be the type of person who often tells little lies that are harmless or even beneficial to you or someone else. It's not uncommon for the person to mix lies and truth to protect or prevent someone from suffering. They are also called prosocial liars, as we discussed earlier. It's important to note that for this person to lie to you, there must be participation on your end.

In other words, most of the time, you might even pick up that the person isn't telling the whole truth, but because you sense the intention is benevolent, you just allow it to pass. Most of the time, white liars are driven by the need to alleviate suffering, disappointment, and hurt for another. So in many cases, they will be kind, empathetic, and compassionate people. Using some of the signals we've discussed throughout this book, such as the speech, tone of voice as well as body language, you should be able to pick up a white lie, especially if you know the person's baseline.

#2. Occasional Liars.

Many of us fall into this category. Rarely we find ourselves lying about something. That would identify us as occasional liars. It doesn't make it a good thing, but at least it's not a regular thing, and for the most part, we feel absolutely devastated by the face.

This type of liar will often feel and demonstrate a lot of guilt, causing them to confess and ask for forgiveness. Most of the time, you will be able to catch an occasional liar (mainly because they suck at it), and they will genuinely apologize and work on changing their ways.

#3. Sociopathic Liars.

Such a person lacks empathy, which already makes him or her very difficult to be in a productive relationship with. Add to that the fact that they don't care about falsifying information and you're standing on dangerous grounds. Most of the narcissists and manipulators tend to be sociopathic liars as well. In a later chapter, we'll talk about how you can protect yourself from such people as they can cause you a lot of harm.

The critical thing to remember with sociopathic liars is that they will do anything to get what they want. Using manipulation and trickery is what they do, and they are incapable of feeling sorry or even guilty if their fictitious stories harm you. I know of many people who have struggled to escape the bonds of narcissists and other types of sociopaths. Hence, I encourage you to learn how to identify this type of liar as quickly as possible because the longer you spend time with them and indulge in their fictitious world, the easier it will be to get thrown out of mental, emotional and physical balance.

#4. Compulsive Liars

Ever had a friend who was always telling you stories of how amazing her life was - yet something didn't quite add up? If so, you were most likely dealing with a compulsive liar. This type of liar is quite easy to spot, especially if you've known them long enough. They also tend to display the most classic lying signals, such as avoiding eye contact, rambling, oversharing, tripping over their words, breaking into a sweat, fake smiling, etc. In fact, many of the ideas we have about liars such as, "liars don't look you in the eye" comes from observing compulsive liars. Professional liars can look you in the eye.

There are two types of compulsive liars you must learn to identify—narcissistic and habitual liars. Narcissistic liars usually have a personality disorder as well. They are known for making up grandiose stories centered around their awesomeness. For example, *last weekend, I didn't come out with you guys because I was busy hooking up with a victoria secret model who took me to a private party on a yacht, and I met Kanye West.* Yeah, right!

This type of person loves to embellish things. It's all about making himself or herself appear like the coolest person in the room, no matter what the situation. Sometimes they might take it too far and put other people down so that they can look good. You might see this with women whereby a narcissistic liar creates a terrible rumor about a girl she's jealous of so that she can appear more appealing to a guy she wants to go out with. Observe any of these characters long enough, and you'll soon catch their narcissistic tendencies and far-fetched stories.

A habitual liar, on the other hand, simply lies all the time. It's just a regular habit they'd developed over time and can't seem to help themselves. Even when it makes no sense to lie, they just do. For example, you meet the person outside Starbucks, holding a takeout coffee and ask what they just ordered. Instead of telling you, they got a regular black coffee; they say it's a latte macchiato. I mean, it makes no sense why they have to lie about every darn thing even the most trivial - but they do!

#5. Pathological Liars.

A pathological liar is actually very good at lying. Identifying this type of liar is quite challenging because their lies generally seem real. Unlike the compulsive liars, pathological liars are pros; it's nearly impossible to catch them in the act. Remember when I said not all liars avoid eye contact? This is an excellent example of where that myth fails. A pathological liar will look you in the eye and lie to your face. But one identifier that you can use is the fact that as they look at you, something will "feel" unnatural. That gaze might just be overly intense or too long. In their determination to appear honest, they might go too far. It could also be that they use language formally instead of the usual way they speak when answering your question. Instead of fidgeting with their fingers or tapping their legs, they might become as still as a rock. These are some red flags you can look out for, and if you spot them in clusters, then be cautious because it could be that you're in the midst of deception.

If you choose to confront any of these liars on their deception, make sure you do it in non-aggressive ways because some of them might overreact in non-productive ways. You never want to make a liar (especially the more dangerous and professional ones) feel embarrassed or threatened as that might make matters worse and put you in unforeseen danger.

Those Who Lie Behind The Safety Of A Screen

This chapter would be incomplete if we didn't mention and prepare you for perhaps the biggest liars you will ever encounter in your life - those hiding behind the screens. Thanks to the Internet, the world has become more connected than ever. Information is transported and communicated across the globe faster than ever before. While this has created a lot of transparency, it has also created a breeding ground for a lot of fake news and Internet liars. Twitter is always trying to fight the fake news that goes viral, politicians seem to be going toe to toe with some version of fake news that was leaked out, and even celebrities are having to deal with it, whether self-manufactured or not.

One of my favorite comedians, "Fluffy," aka Gabriel Iglesias shared one such event during one of his Netflix Specials. He shared how not too long ago someone wrote an article online that went viral where they pronounced the comedian dead. Soon after the story spread all over social media, the news media picked it up, and people actually started believing that fluffy was, in fact, dead. Martin (his trusted partner in crime) caught the news and quickly called fluffy to find out if there was any truth behind the news. Of course, fluffy responded, "no man. I'm not dead!" Of course, it's way funnier when he tells the story, so check out that Netflix special if you're up for some fake news comedy. But in all seriousness, liars are in abundance online, and for some reason, fake news tends to go really viral. So just because you see something on Twitter or reported on local news broadcast doesn't mean it's true.

While I do believe that majority of the people are well intended and generally tell the truth, it's better to be safe than sorry. So audit where you get your news. Audit who you communicate with online and watch out for any red flags when they text or email you. If you like getting into chat rooms and live forums, try not to be naive. Not everyone on the other end of the device is as truthful as you. The Internet is full of tricksters, grifters, and outright liars of every kind. Some are harmless, while others are full-blown narcissists and pathological liars. You need to protect yourself and stay safe while communicating and consuming information online.

Most liars on the Internet today will tend to write impersonally when reporting something, and they will often mismatch the use of their present and past tense. If it's an article you are reading online, you might also notice there is no time stamp on the piece of information even though it's supposed to be hot news. They might also claim to be broadcasting researched information yet provide no further verification or source. Sometimes people might leave out important facts or distort certain facts to influence the narrative of a story, especially on media. That's why you need to look deeper and figure out the whole context. If you notice there's an outrage and a story is evoking strong emotions from you or others, that's a red flag that you need to research that piece of information further. Get curious about its source before making a sound judgment about whether it is good or bad. Remember the Internet news has a tendency to work like that old game of telephone. Each time someone retweets or rewrites something, there's a high chance important information will get lost, and some embellishment will be added to make the new post more "clickbaity" and to rally up opinions. So if you have an emotional reaction online, whether you're chatting with someone, reading a message, email, or blog from someone or news update, become aware the moment strong emotional reactions are triggered. That should be the red flag that causes you to tread carefully because, on many occasions, the information you're being presented with has been designed to make you fall into that emotional rollercoaster where nothing good ever results.

One more piece of advice I'd like to give you is to slow down and think about the information that's presented to you online before jumping into any conclusion. Sometimes we can see only half of the information and misinterpret it or miss the context that would otherwise alter its meaning. It's not just about catching fake news; it's about discerning and finding the truth. That requires thinking and a strong ability to read between the lines.

Chapter 08: Speed-Reading People

While you are not going to become a mind reader as a result of reading this book, you're going to get to good at analyzing and interpreting people's intentions and unspoken words. People might think you a mind reader. We've all wished we could have the astonishing powers that Sherlock Homes possesses of speed reading people down to the details of whom they slept with last night. That's not quite what you'll get here in this chapter. Instead, what you'll have is a framework for mastering this art form. The more you practice it, the better and more accurate you'll become. But it can't be a wild goose chase. Speed reading people is not about guessing. It's about using common sense that is backed by scientific research and understanding of human behavior. There are five main research-based things you need to concern yourself with if you wish to speed read the person in front of you: context, clusters, culture, baseline, personal bias.

How To Read People

If you want to read people more accurately, there are specific errors you must avoid and certain aspects to bear in mind when making your analysis. You also need to read people using all your senses, not just your eyes or ears. Here are the five discussed in better detail.

• Get a baseline to read the person.
If you don't know how a person operates under normal, non-threatening conditions, then you're just guessing with your analysis. Different people behave differently, and it would be

hard to speed-read someone and conclude they are deceiving you if you don't know how they usually act. Some people are just naturally jumpy, or they stutter. So that doesn't tell you anything. However, if a nervous person suddenly stops moving and becomes as still as a rock - that's definitely a red flag. What you need to ask yourself to read the person better is, "how does this person normally act, and is this body movement part of their normal behavior?"

• Culture. You can't effectively read a person if you don't understand their cultural habits and signals. Worse still, you might end up misinterpreting the cues you're receiving. For example, if you're talking to a Latin man and they are standing so close to you that might come off as offensive, but to them, it's their natural behavior. It doesn't mean you any harm. The same goes for eye movement. In Africa, someone will look at you with lowered eyes or not even make eye contact, and if you interpret that as dishonesty, you've just killed the rapport. Therefore you must take the time to educate yourself on language patterns and what they mean depending on the culture you're interacting with. A good question to ask yourself when uncertain is, "what's this individual's cultural heritage, and is this unconscious body signal something normal in their culture?"

• Pay attention to the context or setting. Don't assume that because someone is crossing their arms, they are closed up. If the room is cold or the chair they are sitting in is missing an armrest, it's common sense that they would fold their arms. In such a setting, crossed arms don't relay mean much. Therefore what you need to be asking yourself when you see a particular body posture is "should someone in this setting act or hold themselves in this way?"

• Look for cluster signals. Avoid interpreting and analyzing a person based on one message. If you only look for one telltale sign and assume that's enough to read the person, you'll not excel at this great art. Perhaps in movies that might work, but in real life, you need a lot more than just a fake smile or fidgeting with the hands. Instead, you need to observe a series of actions that almost begin to tell a story of their own. For example, the person starts sweating on the forehead, and the lips in a room that's cool in temperature and they continue to touch their face and stutter or even struggle to speak, as the conversation gets deeper. That might be an indication of deception. So what you need to ask yourself is, "are most of this person's behavior telling a different story from what he or she is saying, and do they associate with deception?"

• Become more aware of your personal biases. If you don't increase awareness of your personal biases, it will be hard to read people right. The fact of the matter is, we are reading people through the lens of our own perceptions. That means if you like or dislike a person, your analysis of that person will be influenced by that perception. When a person compliments you, makes you feel good, appears to be similar to you, or if you find the person attractive, all these things can sway your judgment unconsciously. And if you're going to convince yourself that you're entirely unbiased, well, that's probably the biggest bias of them all! No one expects you to get rid of your bias - just become more aware.

Developing Your Speed Reading

Speed reading is a technique that will help you perfect the art form of reading people. It's fast, and when done right can help you understand how another person is feeling so, you can adapt your message and deal with them more effectively. It's an excellent technique for ensuring effective communication and rapport regardless of the person you're interacting with. It can also help you quickly detect people that are harmful or dangerous to you long before they strike. Just as it is with speed reading a book, speed reading a person is all about practice. But where should you start and what should you be listening and looking for to speed read a person?

A lot of it we have already covered, but let me give you a quick rundown of how you would speed-read someone you're in conversation with. First, you need to create a baseline, as we said previously. That baseline tells you the mannerisms and normal unconscious behavior of the person when they feel comfortable. Observe the breath, body movement, eye movement, hands, and legs to have a holistic understanding of how this person carries themselves as they speak. Notice also their normal tone of voice and cadence as they express themselves about trivial things. Once you have a baseline established, move on to the next thing. Start looking for deviations. What you're trying to spot here are inconsistencies between the baseline you've created and the person's gestures and words. Are there any leaking facial expressions popping up? Has the blinking rate increased? Is the person clearing their throat repeatedly all of a sudden? If you notice inconsistencies, it's a good idea to probe further so you can start gathering data for the next step. That step is observing clusters of gestures. You want to notice what story the non-verbal cues are displaying. Is it consistent with the story the person is saying? For example, I saw an interview with a woman who shot her children and then drove them to the hospital where they eventually succumbed to their wounds. During an interview, the woman who was trying hard to show emotional devastation using her words kept leaking fascinating facial expressions and body cues that actually told a different story. Her words were those of grief, but her face showed no sign of it, and every so often, one could spot something that resembled a smile or grin. The description of the frightful state of her children also didn't water her eyes one bit, and she seemed to be extremely still (almost like a rock) as she described the loss of her children. In such a situation, it is easy to find clusters of gestures that tell a very different story from what the person is speaking with words. That is what you need to find, as well. When you do, proceed with caution because chances are, you're witnessing deception in motion.

The next step to help you speed-read a person is to observe how they walk and how the person continues to interact with other people in the group or around you. Does the expression change? What about posture and body language? You should also listen attentively to the words they choose, their pitch, and how strong their voice is. The main thing you want to observe, especially when not sure if someone is trying to deceive you, is a cluster of these four gestures recurring over and over again. These are hand touching, face touching, crossing arms, and leaning away. Individually none of these cues imply deception, but when expressed together, they tell a very intriguing story that you need to be wary of.

5 Techniques To Speed Read People

#1. Notice their outward appearance.

There's a lot of non-verbal communication being passed on just from the way someone dresses. Pay attention to their clothing. For example, a neat and formal appearance tells you the person is conscientious. Narcissists tend to put too much care into their appearance and probably show a bit more muscle (for men) or cleavage (for women) than you and I would care for. Also, take note of their facial expression and whether they are smiling or frowning, etc.

#2. Motions.

Another technique to speed read is to observe their overall body movement and hand motions. Are there gestures being used that convey a particular message you should be aware of? For example, is the person of American culture and yet shaking his head side to side (which for us indicates a negative) while speaking of something positive? That inconsistency can be a red flag that you need to continue observing to see if a cluster of them show up.

#3. Listen attentively to their paralinguistics.

By this, I mean digging deeper into how the person is using the tool of language as well as his voice to communicate. Is it a strong voice? Is it a high pitch of is the voice deepening? Does it sound natural? What about the cadence? The more you use this technique, the easier it will be to pick up the real meaning behind common statements such as "I'm fine" or "it's okay." Many parents are very good at telling when their child is lying from the simple response of "I'm telling the truth," and that's partly due to the fact that they use this technique subconsciously to pick up on the inconsistency of the child's mannerism.

#4. Take notice of the mirrored body language between the two of you. Mirror neurons are built-in monitors in our brain that reflect other people's state of mind. We are naturally wired to read each other's body language, so this is a great technique to use to determine how the other person is feeling. A smile from the other person will automatically activate smile muscles in your face, and so will a frown. If a person likes you, they will likely have arched eyebrows, and you'll notice their facial muscles relaxing and the head tilting a bit. You might also notice something similar happening within your body as well, which creates a reciprocal movement between the two of you. If, however, your partner doesn't reciprocate that behavior as you initiate it, the person could be sending a message that they don't resonate with you.

#5. Look for immediate or apparent personality clues to help you identify what kind of person you're dealing with. For example, does the person appear to be more introverted or extroverted? How relaxed does he or she look? Is the person more of a thinker or a feeler? What kind of action words do they like using? How much space do they like to have between you?

Using these techniques to analyze people will require a lot of practice so don't be hasty in your judgment and allow yourself a large sample size before proclaiming yourself a speed-reading expert. Don't forget, liars try more, and they tend to be very uncomfortable with silence, so the more present and unbiased you are, the easier it will be to quickly and accurately speed read someone and identify their real intention.

Chapter 09: Are You Emotionally Intelligent?

Emotional intelligence plays a significant role in your ability to analyze people and also create meaningful relationships.

What Does it Mean to be Emotionally Intelligent?

John D Mayer, Ph.D., a personality analyst who wrote a paper in the 90s around the subject of emotional intelligence, describes it as the capacity to reason about emotions and sensitive information. One of the reasons emotional intelligence matters is that the higher your levels of EI (emotional intelligence), the easier it will be to accurately and quickly solve a variety of emotionally related problems. You can easily spot and interpret body language signals and facial expressions, which is extremely vital to becoming great at analyzing people. The more you can understand people, what motivates them, what non-verbal cues they are communicating, etc., the easier it will be to build rapport.

Raising Your Emotional Intelligence

If you want to raise your emotional intelligence which is something highly recommended for anyone who wants to get better at reading people, I encourage you to work on increasing the following:

• Your self-awareness. It is perhaps one of the fundamentals of developing your emotional intelligence, yet few take the time to learn how to increase self-awareness. Evaluate your emotions. Tune into your true feelings. Pay attention to how you feel as you go about your day and interact with others and notice how that reflects on your verbal and non-verbal communication. Do it without judgment so you can understand your baseline. The main elements of self-awareness are emotional awareness and self-confidence. Emotional awareness is your ability to recognize the emotions that dominate your day and how they affect your body, mind, and affairs. Self-confidence is how you value yourself. How high or low is your self-esteem? How capable do you generally believe you are to do or accomplish things that matter to you? For example, how confident are you that you can accurately analyze and speed read people now that you're learning this topic? Are you still going to doubt your abilities?

• Your motivation. It consists of your drive to improve or meet a set standard that you've chosen, your commitment, initiative, and optimism that will enable you to keep pushing forward until the goal is achieved. To do this well, you need to become aware of your current predisposition. Does your mind automatically rest on a negative or positive attitude? How often are negative thoughts lurking in your mind? How much bias do you carry around with you? Once you know what motivates you and what your mental attitude is, you can adjust it to work more in your favor.

• Your self-control. That is a tough one for many people. Most of us are ruled by our emotions instead of controlling them. Regardless of how powerful a feeling is, you do have power over it, whether negative or positive. By developing your emotional intelligence, you can better control your emotions and even help to release those unwanted ones faster. Instead of being stuck in anger, anxiety, or depression, emotional intelligence enables you to process and get rid of them before much harm occurs. It also helps you to control your temperament better when interacting with people who enjoy "pushing your buttons."

• Empathy. Increasing self-awareness is also about developing empathy - a very crucial ingredient for reading people accurately. What is empathy? The ability to recognize how someone else is feeling. As you get better at discerning the feelings behind others' signals, you will not only know whether someone is truthful or not, but you'll also increase your ability to control the messages you send them.

• Your social skills. Last but not least, increasing your emotional intelligence and awareness powerfully impacts your social skills. You are more equipped to understand others, discern their feelings, needs, and wants. You gain the ability to influence, lead, inspire, and clearly communicate with others, both verbally and non-verbally. In essence, you become the kind of guy or girl that people enjoy being around.

As you can see, developing your emotional intelligence and increasing self-awareness has rewards that surpass being able to read people. It places you at a whole different level and, of course, gives you the superpower of quickly and accurately understanding the person you're interacting with. How well you do in life and business has a lot to do with your level of emotional intelligence, according to researchers. Therefore, in addition to reading this book, I encourage you to study materials that can help you enhance your emotional intelligence.

9 Signs That You Have High Emotional Intelligence

If you are currently working on increasing your emotional intelligence and desire to know if you're on the right track, here are signs that prove beyond a shadow of a doubt that you are a person with high levels of emotional intelligence.

#1. You regularly pause to pay attention to your feelings.

#2. You demonstrate a lot of empathy and understand how other people feel. That enables you to see things through their eyes instead of merely judging them.

#3. You have exceptional social skills and quickly build rapport, nurture relationships, and resolve conflict.

#4. You are comfortable and willing to discuss emotions and sensitivity feelings with others. That means you are open to sharing how you are feeling (i.e., being vulnerable without being weak), and you also have the aptitude for listening to another share his or her feelings.

#5. You can self-regulate your emotions. That includes being able to pause and think through your actions and feelings before outwardly reacting. Your ability to create a buffer time for yourself to think and process your inner state helps you stay calm and cool even in unpleasant situations. In essence, you are in tune with how you feel, but you don't allow your emotions to rule your life.

#6. You're flexible and adaptable to change. Instead of fighting and resisting change, you prefer to flex and sway. That doesn't mean you give up on what you want; it just means you're able to keep your eye on the main vision, adjust where needed without fretting about the detours along the path.

#7. You are authentic. That means you say what you mean and you mean what you say. You live by strong values and principles above all else, and everyone around you sees this demonstrated through character and the way you lead your life.

#8. You offer praise generously and take criticism positively. Because you understand human beings crave appreciation, recognition, and acknowledgment, you freely offer praise and compliments where appropriate. On the same token, you are open-minded enough to take criticism or negative feedback because you see this as a chance to learn more about yourself and the other. As you receive both negative and positive feedback, you still keep your emotions and check. When it is negative, you first attempt to figure out if there is truth to the message by doing a self-analysis.

#9. You have developed the ability to protect yourself from emotional manipulators and even emotional self-sabotage. Your increased self-awareness enables you to see the dark side of having this skill. You know that ill-intentioned people are always lurking about and so you know how to spot them quickly and protect yourself from such individuals. On the same token, you are continuously working on yourself to ensure you don't go over to the dark side and attempt to use this power to manipulate others for your own selfish desires. That's why you continue to work on developing your emotional intelligence and increasing your self-awareness so you can always be protected and secure from the dark influence of this power.

Chapter 10: Protecting Yourself Against Dark Influence And Manipulation

As we mentioned in the last chapter, emotional intelligence can help you protect yourself from others who are trying to manipulate you, and it can also make you aware of when you're using your developed skills in a non-ethical way. This chapter is meant to help you fully understand why you need to protect yourself both against the urge of going dark as well as avoiding those that are already consciously shadowy manipulators. To do it well, we must give some attention to what manipulation and influence mean. Influence is the ability one has to affect or change something or someone. When you can cause someone to replace an action, idea, perception, or behavior, you are influencing him or her. If you were having a conversation with a spouse of lover about whether to watch an action movie this weekend (which you love) or try out a new supposedly romantic restaurant, that's a five-mile drive (which you'd rather not do), influence will come into play. Whoever gets their way will be considered more influential in this case. Manipulation, on the other hand, is exerting shrewd or devious influence for your own selfish gain. Usually, one isn't even thinking about how that particular move will affect the other party. I consider this to be the negative side of influence. When influence is driven by ego and vanity and where self-awareness and empathy are lacking, influence tends to go dark and morph into manipulation.

How Does Dark Influence And Manipulation Work?

The term influence itself is quite neutral and natural to us. However, it can become positive or negative, depending on who is using this technique. The negative side of influence, as I said, is manipulation. It is also coercion, which is pretty much rooted in the same dark nature. Dark influence and manipulation are all around us. It is used in commercials, sales, online advertising, and even between friends and family members. I fell victim to this type of manipulation years ago as I shared in my story, and though there was no physical harm done, the psychological and financial consequences incurred hurt for a long time. Most of the time, manipulative tactics are used in the form of lying, love flooding (i.e., false compliments, buttering someone up to get something out of them), love denial (i.e., starving someone of affection and attention), withdrawal or what's referred to as the silent treatment, reverse psychology and semantic manipulation. There are more ways to manipulate, but I hope you're starting to get an idea of how manipulation is dished out and the kind of tactics to watch out for.

A Peek In The Head Of These Malicious People

What kind of people do you suppose enjoy manipulation, coercion, and dark influence? Sociopaths, narcissists, politicians, some ill-intentioned salespeople, public speakers, attorneys, and any other group of selfish people who simply don't care about anything or anyone else. All they want is to get what they want at any cost and by any means necessary. Sometimes it can even be a girlfriend who is dead set on trapping a man and getting married to him. It can also be a mother who is overly protective of her only son and thinks no woman is good enough for her baby boy. There's no end to the different types of people who either consciously or unconsciously start to practice manipulation.

Have you ever wondered what's going on in the head of such a person? Why lie, deceive, manipulate or coerce someone, especially if you claim to love the person? Well, that's a tough one to answer because some have developed this habit and character as a defense mechanism. Others have been traumatized and are yet to recover, and others simply struggle to express themselves in the right manner. While many will argue that some people are born pure evil, this isn't scientifically proven, and I genuinely feel that behind every manipulator, is a root cause because no one is inherently purely bad. It must have started from somewhere. While this book isn't meant to diagnose the origin of dark influencers and manipulators, I do want to help you develop a discerning eye so you can take appropriate action before they suck you into their dark realm.

Developing A Discerning Eye

Manipulative people are often very toxic. They also tend to be judgmental and have trouble taking responsibility for their own feelings. Instead, they will project their issues onto you. They also exhibit a lot of discrepancies in their communication and behavior. When it comes to getting what they want from you, they can change in a split of a second. For example, someone can go from being nice to nasty and then shift to condescending just so they can get their way.

If you come across someone who just makes you feel strange and frequently uses humor to insult you or others in the room, you're likely dealing with a toxic person. But perhaps the best telltale sign you will spot as you analyze this person is how much they lie. Manipulators just can't seem to help themselves. They will voice assumptions about your intentions or beliefs and then reframe them in a way that makes you look like the bad guy. They are also very good at alienating people and belittling others.

5 Ways To Protect Yourself

#1. Avoid direct and aggressive forms of confrontation. Manipulators are so good at what they do. It won't be too long before the tables are turned, and you end up apologizing for something you haven't done. Trying to convince a manipulator to own their mistakes or to apologize or even feel sorry about what they did sincerely - is a waste of time. It will only lead to arguments and more hurt.

#2. Physically and emotionally distance yourself from a manipulator the moment you identify one. Listen, if you're at a party and five minutes into a conversation, you realize the girl is lying and trying to manipulate you into doing something, get as far away from her as you can. Don't even try to "handle the situation" just find your exit and move on!

#3. Don't take their words or actions personally. Trust me, they will make you feel guilty, wrong, less than, etc. It's what they do. Don't take it personally because most of the negativity these people project are simply projections of what's going on inside them.

#4. Learn to manage your energy and emotions better, so you don't get sucked into their world. The more self-awareness and self-regulation you practice, the easier it will be to develop that buffer time needed to make sure you pause, step away from that setting and liberate yourself from the manipulator.

#5. Set clear boundaries and use clear communication when you communicate with a manipulator. Sometimes you might be forced to deal with someone you already identify is toxic or manipulative. In such cases where it is unavoidable, make the integration as brief as possible, do not share sensitive information that they might use against you, and always say what you mean directly to them and as clearly as possible. This will reduce any chance of exaggeration and conflict, which they often love to create.

Chapter 11: More On People With Dark Personality

Dark influencers, jerks, manipulators, and toxic people are not the only ones you need to protect yourself from. There are also those who are downright evil and enjoy creating trouble for people around them. There are also those who are criminals and take advantage of people or physically hurt them as a way of making a living. These are all people you want to be able to spot as quickly as possible so you can remove yourself from those sticky and dangerous situations.

Know Who You Are Facing Against

If you meet a person in a bar (like I did the woman who ended up ripping me off) or a cocktail party who is there with a hidden agenda (to con, rob, rip off or take advantage of someone), you need to recognize that. I hope that this book has made you more alert and self-aware to the point where you can pick up that body language that raises red flags. People who are criminals, for example, don't require you to try to negotiate or even call them out in public when you spot their lies and manipulative acts. That could turn really bad, really fast. They will tend to react aggressively, harm you, or someone around you, and the whole situation can quickly get out of hand. My suggestion is that you only call someone out on his or her deception when you actually know the person and understand the entire situation. For example, if you're having a conversation with a friend and you realize they are lying to you or trying to be devious, sure call them out on it because you know it will probably just cause them to lash out and nothing more. However, if you're in a new environment, you don't know how deep that deception goes or how many people are involved. Calling out one person could jeopardize your safety even more. Besides, the person might overreact and pull out a knife or gun in anger, and that would be a lot harder to resolve. It's best to focus on analyzing people, discerning truth, and removing yourself and your loved ones from environments and people that seem to threaten your safety.

Spotting a Person with Condescending Attitude

Have you noticed how certain people (especially liars and manipulators) tend to feel more superior to the rest of us and have no trouble making us aware that we are below them? I find that the more someone is faking their "story" or their confidence, success, or intention, the more likely they are to be condescending. People who have issues tend to bring people down to cover up for their own sense of inferiority. Avoid such people whenever possible. A quick way to know if someone has a condescending attitude is to observe his or her body language. Usually, the chin will be up, the forehead will be pulled back, and he or she will likely speak in the third person. You might also notice an emphasis on certain words such as my (when the person is talking about an accomplishment), or they will slow down their words as if they are speaking to a non-intelligent child. Everything is set up to show that they are more superior than you. While condescending people are not necessarily physically dangerous or evil, engaging with such people is very detrimental to your mental well being so I encourage you to train yourself to spot them and make your exit as soon as possible.

Before A Pickpocket Gets To You

The last type of lousy character you need to spot quickly, especially in our modern world, is the classic pickpocket. It is especially important if you live in a big city or frequent events with large crowd gatherings. There are over 400,000 cases of reported pickpocketing taking place every day across the globe. Cities like Florence, Athens, Buenos Aires, Madrid, and others are considered hot spots for pickpocketing. Most of the time, the pickpocketing is taking place in public transportation, museums, train stations, restaurants, bars, beaches, markets, retail stores, and coffee shops. That's mainly because half the time when you're in such an environment your guard is probably down, especially as a tourist in a foreign land. I mean, who isn't relaxed and chilled at the beach? Well, you need to make sure you're always guarded and on the lookout for these people who are constantly looking for easy targets. Use the body language reading techniques to pick up any red flags when you're out and about. Watch out for people who are fidgeting, moving around nervously, or unnecessarily bumping into you. But the best advice I can give, especially if you travel to Europe for vacation or business, is to avoid carrying your best stuff to public places or crowded areas. If you are traveling on public transport with bags, make sure your hands cling tightly to your belongings as the mode of transport slows down to approach stops. Watch your personal zone as much as possible. We already discussed proxemics in an earlier chapter. Go back and read that section again so you can imprint it in your mind and allow it to alert you whenever someone gets too close even if it's Europe where social distancing is different than here. If you come across someone who is really attempting to enter your personal space and get intimate, even if to hand you their phone so you can take their picture, be hyper-aware of your pockets and bags as this might be a distraction. For men, it is also advisable to use a zippered wallet or wrap a rubber band around the wallet to prevent pickpockets from reaching in and pulling out cash or credit cards before you can stop them.

Chapter 12: Using Body Language To Become The Person You Want To Be

Mastering the art of reading and analyzing people has some great benefits. It helps you protect yourself against harm as we just discussed in the last two chapters, it keeps you in control of your interactions with others, and it also does something incredible for you. It makes you a highly effective communicator. You are able to build rapport, resolve conflicts, and nurture the relationships that matter to you. In short, it makes you become a better version of yourself. What many of us don't realize when we pick up material like this to educate ourselves on how to read others is that by doing that, we also learn to understand ourselves better. We discover ways of becoming more of the individual we have always wanted to be. To make sure that you actually implement all the information you've learned in this book so you can continue to improve yourself and become who you were meant to be, let me remind you of one of the main identifiers that we all subconsciously use to determine how highly we rate someone for the first time - the handshake. As soon as you meet someone for the first time, they will read and make a judgment of you based on your outward appearance, facial expression, and most definitely based on your handshake. So in case you are still unsure about what handshake to develop moving forward, let's devote a little time to that now.

The Best Kind Of Handshake

There are a lot of Do's and Don'ts when it comes to handshakes, and if you remember, I wrote a whole segment on the types of handshakes that are considered awful. Read them once again and make sure you steer clear of them. Instead, what I want to focus on here is the best handshake you can start practicing.

The best handshake that will communicate the right message to the person in front of you involves the palms of both you and the other person positioned vertically. Practice some self-awareness here, and if you realize the presser you are applying is greater or much lesser than the other person, then regulate yourself quickly. Don't offer a submissive or a dominating handshake. Submissive is when your palm is facing up and falls below the palm of the other person. In so doing, you're giving the other person the upper hand. Dominant is the opposite of submissive and indicates to the other person that you want to dominate.

Use the double handler instead. It is considered one of the most potent handshakes in the world. To do it right, you need both hands. First, the person presents you with a palm down thrust, and then you step in and respond with a palm up and apply your second hand to make the palm of the other person straight. Use this handshake, and you will always display the right amount of equality in power and subconsciously send the right message to the other person.

Does Mirroring Work?

We have been using mirror techniques since infancy. Yes, mirroring is a powerful technique, and many of us already do it to some degree, especially with people we are closely connected to.

Mirroring with strangers also works if you do it naturally and with the right rhythm. Done poorly, you just come across looking like a creep. However, when you learn to read the body cues others are sending and use them in subtle ways to mirror back to them what you feel they are experiencing, it is a great way to establish a sense of bond. People will feel like you get them. What this comes down to (assuming you want to do it appropriately) is to practice as much as you can by doing it in a way that feels and seems natural to you. If you imitate or mimic for the sake of being like the other person, it will backfire on you.

For example, if your partner comes to you with a frowning face, mirror back to them a somber look and show concern. That alone will cause them to open up and feel like you understand their needs.

7 Effective Ways to Show Your Confidence

Many studies show that people who appear more confident tend to achieve more success in life. If you want to become who you were meant to be in life, increasing your level of confidence is a must. You can only successfully apply all the knowledge gained in this book if you've got sufficient amounts of confidence; otherwise, you'll continuously doubt yourself, overexert your efforts and end up passing the wrong body language to the people you interact with. Here are seven practical ways you can increase and show that you're a confident person.

#1. Stand up straight with your spine erect, head level, and shoulders relaxed. Good posture is vital to appear confident. People who slouch or carry a misaligned body posture struggle to communicate that they are confident. Make sure you're posture is aligned correctly.

#2. Maintain the right amount of direct eye contact. You don't want your eyes wandering across the room, and you also don't want to stare too long at someone without blinking. Find a perfect cadence with your eye movement that works for you. What you want to aim for is a rapport, almost like a shared dance between you and the person you are addressing.

#3. Avoid fidgeting, and definitely do not tap your feet. There are certain habits we develop over time, such as tapping our feet on the ground (something I've been guilty of), jingling coins in the pocket, twirling the hair (ladies), or too much swaying back and forth. These habits, while harmless, can make you come across as lacking confidence. They also distract the person listening to you and thereby dilute the message you're attempting to communicate.

#4. Avoid placing your hands in your pocket or jacket. Your hands should be visible when addressing someone. Whenever you pocket your hands, it sends off the signal that you're nervous, uncomfortable, and uncertain. To come across as confident, make sure your hands are visible, and your palms face up as much as possible.

#5. Find your strong and powerful voice. The best way to speak in a tone, pitch, and cadence that comes across as powerful and strong is to talk while pressing down firmly on your abdominal muscles. In other words, you want to draw your power from your stomach area. That will ensure it carries more emotional conviction and also lowers the pitch a bit, which makes you project strength. It will take a bit of practice, but the more you do it, the more you will tell the difference between your weak voice and your strong voice.

#6. Carry a positive open body posture and make an effort to be interested instead of impressive. If you want to show confidence, engage with the person in front of you. Immerse yourself in the present moment instead of worrying about yourself, how you look, what you'll say next etc. The more focus you place on the other person, the more they will perceive you as being confident and interesting.

#7. Avoid using filler words. I think this is pretty straightforward. The fewer the filler words you use, such as "um," "like," "uh," and "so," the better. You will come across as more concise and clear in your communication, which will project confidence. I also encourage you to take the time to pronounce your words clearly. People who speak too fast or run through their words often sound nervous and less confident. Be comfortable to address people at a tempo that helps you fully express yourself.

When it comes to showing confidence, there is no magic pill to swallow or shortcut you can take. It comes down to how willing you are to work on yourself daily, improve the aspects of yourself that still need improving, and boldly share with the world your authentic expression. The more you can discover who you really are and authentically share that with the world unapologetically, the easier it will be to convey confidence.

Conclusion

Congratulations on making it all the way to the end of How To Analyze People: A Practical Guide To Analyzing Body Language, Speed Reading People, And Increasing Emotional Intelligence & Protecting Against Dark Influence & Manipulation. We started this journey of understanding what body language means and how to interpret the non-verbal cues people are always sending out with the promise that you would learn the skills and techniques that can enable you to speed read any person and discover their real intention. In so doing, you would be able to protect yourself from ill-intentioned people and also develop the highly necessary skills of effective communication and rapport building. In the process of this, I hope you've realized that analyzing people is great and needed in our modern society, but more important than that is learning how to gain mastery over your own body and life.

Taking full control of your life is the primary purpose of mastering this art because, at the end of the day, the most important person that you need to analyze in your world in order to succeed and have the life of your dreams - is you!

Whether you're a student, businessperson, employee, or parent, picking up this book should help make you an effective communicator and help propel you into greater success.

In this book, you've learned the science behind why the body moves as it does, different body postures, and what the different areas of your body are communicating, including your face, torso, arms, and legs. You also learned to distinguish between good and back handshakes, and I even described how to start doing the handshake right. In addition to the techniques we learned, such as mirroring and posture, to help you build rapport and project confidence, you have also learned how to quickly spot people with malicious intent so you can protect yourself. This book has a lot of information jammed packed into it, so I encourage you to read it more than once and definitely put every chapter to practice if you wish to get the full benefit of this topic.

Now it's your turn to get out into the world and use everything you've learned to improve your life. If there's one thing I expect you to take away from this book is that body language accounts for the majority of our daily communication as human beings. Whether it is an intimate, social, or professional encounter, what your body and the other person's body convey are messages that reveal more truth than the words we speak. From now on, you never need to rely on mere words or miss critical red flags when talking to a stranger. Continue on this path of understanding your body and studying non-verbal communication. You will soon become a master at reading and analyzing people from all walks of life across different cultures.

Resources

Guide to Good Posture. (n.d.). Retrieved May 4, 2020, from https://medlineplus.gov/guidetogoodposture.html

Conner, C. (2018, February 11). How To Spot A Lie In 5 Seconds (And The Biggest Lie I Ever Told In PR). Retrieved May 4, 2020, from https://www.forbes.com/sites/cherylsnappconner/2018/02/10/how-to-spot-a-lie-in-5-seconds-and-why-it-matters-in-pr/#3829f3ff5959

D. (2019, December 4). Eight Types of Lies that People Tell. Retrieved May 4, 2020, from https://www.thehopeline.com/different-kinds-of-lies-you-tell/

M. (2020, April 16). Improving Emotional Intelligence (EQ). Retrieved May 4, 2020, from https://www.helpguide.org/articles/mental-health/emotional-intelligence-eq.htm

Edberg, H. (2019, March 2). 18 Ways to Improve Your Body Language. Retrieved May 4, 2020, from https://www.positivityblog.com/18-ways-to-improve-your-body-language/

HuffPost is now a part of Verizon Media. (n.d.). Retrieved May 4, 2020, from https://www.huffpost.com/entry/the-psychology-of-resting-bitch-face-syndrome-and-what_b_57bd18fce4b07d22cc3a3055

M. (2020a, April 16). Emotional Intelligence Toolkit. Retrieved May 4, 2020, from https://www.helpguide.org/articles/mental-health/emotional-intelligence-toolkit.htm

Guide to Good Posture. (n.d.-b). Retrieved May 4, 2020, from https://medlineplus.gov/guidetogoodposture.html

WIRED. (2019, May 21). Former FBI Agent Explains How to Read Body Language | Tradecraft | WIRED. Retrieved May 4, 2020, from https://www.youtube.com/watch?v=4jwUXV4QaTw

M. (2020c, April 16). Nonverbal Communication. Retrieved May 4, 2020, from https://www.helpguide.org/articles/relationships-communication/nonverbal-communication.htm

Lightning Source UK Ltd.
Milton Keynes UK
UKHW022219110822
407202UK00010B/119